Balancing Act

Balancing Act

*Reflections, Meditations, and Coping
Strategies for Today's Fast-Paced Whirl*

ADELE RYAN MCDOWELL, PH.D.

BALBOA.
PRESS
A DIVISION OF HAY HOUSE

Balboa Press books may be ordered through booksellers or by contacting:

Balboa Press
A Division of Hay House
1663 Liberty Drive
Bloomington, IN 47403
www.balboapress.com
1-(877) 407-4847

Because of the dynamic nature of the Internet, any Web addresses or links contained in this book may have changed since publication and may no longer be valid. The views expressed in this work are solely those of the author and do not necessarily reflect the views of the publisher, and the publisher hereby disclaims any responsibility for them.

Some of the essays in this book were originally published in the author's column "wavelength" on United Press International's Religion and Spirituality website from 2006 through 2009. The following pieces have been edited, restructured, and, in some cases, renamed for use in this book: "Mr. Toad's wild ride"; "The enchanted forest of puzzlement"; "Pop! goes attention"; "An emotional hangover"; "Balance"; "The gods want you for a meeting"; "Got stress?"; "Healing the violent heart"; "How does one live with death?" and "50 ways to feed your soul." "Flight grounded" and "Houston, we have lift-off " were originally published as one piece titled "The long, nervous slog to enlightenment." "Hardwired for connection" was originally published as "The 10 spiritual lessons of relationships." "Being resilient" was originally published as "Hey, it's scary out there." "Balance" was originally titled "Springing into balance." "Unleashing the soul" was originally published as "Six ways to free your soul."

The author of this book does not dispense medical advice or prescribe the use of any technique as a form of treatment for physical, emotional, or medical problems without the advice of a physician, either directly or indirectly. The intent of the author is only to offer information of a general nature to help you in your quest for emotional and spiritual well-being. In the event that you use any of the information in this book for yourself, which is your constitutional right, the author and the publisher assume no responsibility for your actions.

Cartoons used with permission, page 1 © Mischa Richter/The New Yorker Collection/www.cartoonbank.com; pages 33, 63, 89, and 105 © Charles Barsotti/The New Yorker Collection/www.cartoonbank.com.

Cover photograph © D. Sharon Pruitt, Pink Sherbet Photography, used with permission. Photograph of the author courtesy Paul McDermott Photography.

ISBN: 978-1-4525-3216-5 (sc)
ISBN: 978-1-4525-3217-2 (e)
Library of Congress Control Number: 2001012345

Printed in the United States of America
Balboa Press rev. date: 02/03/2011

For my sister, Anne,
the funniest person I know
and my best gift ever

Contents

Start, Stop, and Stalled

Monkey Minds and Tender Hearts

Easy Does It

Natural Rhythms

Helpful Strategies

Prologue

Have you heard this one? A woman goes to her priest and says, "Father, Father, please pray for my therapist." The priest asks, "Why, my child?" The woman answers, "I am in therapy one hour a week, but my therapist is there all week long."

That one always makes me smile because there is some truth to it. Many therapists have reached their side of the desk after years of personal excavation and inner work. Many have been motivated by their own chaotic backgrounds to search for meaning and understanding. Many have discovered along the way that they have an innate affinity and sensitivity for the work. I am no exception to that general rule.

I came to my work as a psychotherapist after years in business. It was my dream to sit in one-to-one consultations with people. I remember leading my first clinic client into my cubbyhole office and closing the thin door. I was the happiest woman alive. I had achieved my dream. I was a counselor!

It took me a few years to realize that I had actually

been doing similar work in my corporate career. People are people, and the relationship issues, personality quirks, and deep questions do not disappear in the workplace. In fact, I learned, some time later, that in one position I held, Human Resources was sending me all the problem employees. Who knew that was my first unofficial seven-year internship? It was excellent, unintentional training. In retrospect, I believe that the gods had lined up everything in perfect order to prepare me for my future work in psychotherapy.

Let's go back to the young woman asking for prayers for her therapist. The joke fits; I have needed all the tools, help, and tricks of the trade to work on creating balance in my life. Finding balance has been my holy grail. Decades of talking to people have taught me that I am not alone in this pursuit.

The world is fast, and time seems to have accelerated. I have heard it said that our 24-hour days are really more like 16 hours. I don't know if there is any real science behind that statement, but it certainly feels that way.

Further, we live in the information age. We are bombarded constantly with new stimuli, facts, data, and technology. It has been said, anecdotally speaking, that the amount of new information made available every five minutes in today's world is the equivalent to the entire body of knowledge during the Renaissance. Doesn't that give you pause?

If that idea seems too far-fetched, consider how technology has opened up almost every frontier. We are neighbors with people across the globe. Everything is accessible, and often instantly so. Technology allows us to go backward—think carbon dating and DNA testing—and can leapfrog us forward. For example, medicine, communications, and electronics are moving ahead at breakneck speeds. No sooner do you understand how to work your cell phone than it is time to update your gadget, and you have a whole new learning curve with an even faster, multimodal, superfunctioning personal electronic device.

Life is fast and crazy-busy. We all need balance just so we can stay afloat and find neutral. Both physically and psychologically, when we maintain balance, we don't tip over. We are less reactive to whatever comes our way.

Remember Louis Pasteur, the father of pasteurization? When Pasteur was very ill, he reasoned that if he could find balance, he could heal. He instructed his lab assistants to go to the river and bring him buckets of sun-warmed sand. He recalled that, as a child, he had accompanied his mother to the river when she did the family's washing. Pasteur would play contentedly with the sand on the riverbank; everything was right in his world. When his assistants returned with the requested buckets of sand, Pasteur plunged his hands and feet into the sand to consciously recall the childhood experiences that had brought him peace and contentment. By replicating these experiences as an adult, he not only regained balance, he healed.

Research in the field of psychoneuroimmunology, or mind-body medicine, has taught us that all parts of us—mind, body, and spirit—are connected and influence one another. Emotions, thoughts, bodily sensations, and yearnings of the soul work hand in hand within us. It stands to reason that we would need a holistic approach if we are to find balance.

In this book you will find reflections, meditations, and coping strategies grounded in psychoneuroimmunology, cognitive-behavioral, transpersonal, and positive psychologies, and big-picture spirituality to help take you through the day—and even the night.

Urban legend

A woman is in her yard, and a well-fed, well-cared-for dog—complete with tags—approaches her. She pats the dog's head; the dog follows her into her house, walks down the hall, and finds a corner, where it promptly takes a nap. After an hour or so, the dog wakes up, stretches, and goes to the door, waiting to be let out of the house. This event repeats itself for a few days. Growing more and more curious about this dog, the woman of the house decides to write a note, which she attaches to the dog's collar. The note reads, "Your dog comes to my house every afternoon to take a nap." The next day the dog returns with a note attached to his collar. This note says, "This dog comes from a house with six children, two of whom are under three years of age. He is trying to catch up on his sleep. Can I come with him tomorrow?"

Start, Stop, and Stalled

"Can you describe this china shop?"

Acceleration

The days go faster and the weeks blur; before you know it, another month is about to end. Resolutions for a better life, physical fitness, more balance, and a new savings plan have been shelved or forgotten. You seem to get busier and busier with each passing year. Your life has accelerated. Someone pushed the fast-forward button and forgot to tell you.

At first you can manage the pace. In fact, you feel quite pleased with yourself at the agility with which you handle all the incoming. You are on top of your game. Your mind is firing on all four cylinders; your thoughts are clear and cogent. You are making tracks. All is good.

Without warning, the pace seems to accelerate exponentially. You miss a few details, put off an important task, and manage a quick last-minute save. No one really notices, but you feel somewhat embarrassed and ashamed about the near miss and potential disasters. You are convinced that if you just work a bit harder you can be operating at peak performance once again. A few late nights, a couple of catch-up weekends, and you are certain you can reclaim your solid grip on the matters at hand.

Over time, the demands ratchet up to a new level. Extra hours become the new norm. Your home life suffers; you eat in gulps—and mostly sweet and salty. There is no time for exercise or socializing. You begin to fray around the edges. Your fuse is short; you are overtired and totally stressed. Seemingly overnight, your life is all about work. You become a whirling dervish of activity, spinning yourself into tighter and tighter coils.

Do you recognize the accelerated spin?

Habits are first cobwebs, then cables.
Spanish proverb

Runaway brain

It's been one of those weeks, crazy beyond belief. You are so, so tired, and you can't wait to climb into your warm, soft bed. You have made it through the day with the promise of a good night's sleep. That promise was your solace as you marched through the day's drills and completed your routines. It has served as a balm that has filled you with anticipatory comfort.

You complete your nocturnal ablutions and ready yourself for sleep. You slide beneath the covers, adjust the pillows, assume your favorite sleeping position, and prepare to fall asleep. Your body is desperate for rest. Maybe you get a sliver of sleep, or maybe the engines have already revved up and you can hear the faint roar in the distance. It is the sound of your runaway brain, like a fully loaded freight train hurtling through the night; it is beginning to pick up speed and momentum as it roars into your awakened head.

Your body is ready to fall asleep, but your mind is wide awake and alert, pacing the perimeter of your consciousness. Your brain is busily creating scenarios, plotting strategies, adding to your to-do list, and juggling your doubts and fears. Those doubts and fears are like sponges that expand in the dark; they grow large and unwieldy and send your body into a state of hypervigilance. Sleep is an enigma to you. You are awake. You are alert, and you are now in wait for any new worry or concern to rattle your thoughts as the old ones bang incessantly inside your skull to familiar staccato rhythms.

This is a long, scary night. You know you have to ride it out, but you are furious that it has come to this. You work hard to disengage from the internal chatter; you focus on simple pleasures, loving moments, and all things positive to anesthetize the negative. Yet your overloaded brain chugs relentlessly. You wait for it run out of steam so that you can surrender to the comfort of sleep.

Be gentle with yourself. It happens from time to time.

Sleep is the best meditation.
The Dalai Lama

I'm for whatever gets you through the night.
Frank Sinatra

Mr. Toad's wild ride

Are you stressed? In fact, are you so stressed that you feel you have created a new, high-intensity, off-the-Richter-scale level of stress? Have you been stretched out of your comfort zone to catch fly balls from the universe? Do you feel pelted by incoming, not-so-charming surprises, like snowballs from hell? Do you feel pressed to do more, be more, accept more than you ever thought possible?

If so, welcome to Mr. Toad's wild ride.

You see, Mr. Toad will take you on an ever-changing adventure of constant movements that stretch your internal resources, call forth all your reservoirs of wherewithal, and force you to be slammed back into your whole self. This is, to borrow a phrase, where the rubber meets the road. You are on a forward trajectory; there is no turning back.

Mr. Toad's wild ride breaks the sound barrier of limitation. This wild ride catapults you into change.

The rules for riding Mr. Toad are fairly simple. It's akin to riding a surfboard. You stand up and anchor your feet. You bend your knees (therein lies the flexibility to ride the ups and downs of the incoming); you balance your weight (and this calls for being *in* your body, not operating solely from the shoulders up and allowing only your mind to call the shots); and you pay attention to what's coming toward you. If you get washed out (read: overwhelmed, overloaded, or shut down), you simply get up, reanchor, rebalance, refocus, and begin anew.

It sounds easy enough, but it is actually quite the feat. There are no seat belts or restraints. It takes a fair amount of guts to hang on to Mr. Toad as you are tossed and turned and somersaulted through psychic space.

Congratulate yourself for your ability to handle Mr. Toad's wild ride.

I try to take it one day at a time, but lately several days have attacked me at once.

Anonymous

Unable to drive

Ever have one of those days when you feel like you just can't get started? Your brain doesn't engage, your body is stuck on idle, and you can't seem to get on track with the roster of daily duties. It's as if your motor won't turn over and is unable to catch. There is no spark, no spontaneous combustion. There is no connection to start your engine.

More often than not, you meet this state of body-mind with irritation and frustration. You have things to do and goals to meet, and this state of inertia is getting you nowhere. You don't have the oomph to get off the couch. Staring into space seems as vigorous as you can be at this moment. You look at the clock and groan. There are things you have to do. Yet your body-mind is totally uncooperative and completely stalled. You are going nowhere fast.

In an effort to jump-start the process, you think caffeine, loads and loads of caffeine, or, perhaps, some protein, a good breakfast or some of last night's leftovers. Then there is sugar; you ferret out the cookies. By God, you are going to get your body-mind in gear if it's the last thing you do. However, over the past few months there have been too many jump-starts. You have withdrawn from the well one too many times. Your system has temporarily shut down.

You could spend the better part of the day bemoaning the fact that you can't get done what you have to do. Or you might consider the radical thought of listening to what your body-mind might want to do. Leisurely read the paper over a second cup of coffee? Take a walk around the neighborhood? Go back to bed? Tinker in the garden? Watch *Law & Order* reruns? Take a mental health day?

Here's the irony: If you stop and listen to your body-mind and give it what it wants, for an hour or even a day, you will find that you can restart your engine. Not only will you be able to re-engage, you will find yourself with more physical stamina and mental energy. You changed directions; you were no longer driving down the same road at breakneck speed. You took a break; now you can get behind the wheel and continue your journey.

A good rest is half the work.

Yugoslavian proverb

Re-entry

Have you been away from your regular routine? Have you enjoyed a vacation, a long weekend—or even a day—to call your own? Can you recall the sheer glee of non-ordinary time when the day stretches out before you full of promise and pleasure? The hours buck structure and routine. The constraints of everyday duties give way to expansive possibilities or the sweet relief of doing nothing. It's as if you have been freed from the boxed world of your existence. The hours unfold easily. Your options are unlimited. You can zoom around in a happy dance, doing what you love or exploring new adventures. You may choose to zone out and stare at the horizon or swing back and forth in a hammock as you surf your dreams. You have time to call your own, and you are rich with options. Life is good.

Then, with surprising celerity, the alarm rings and your downtime is over. You return to the familiar work demands, school schedules, meetings, volunteer training, and the like. Life falls into the rhythm of daily patterns.

Sometimes the shift from downtime to ordinary time is a challenge. You feel that you are trying to squeeze yourself back into a box, albeit a box that you have chosen and created.

Your re-entry is anything but easy. You are reluctant to give up your newfound freedoms and simple pleasures. You want to maintain some of the sanity and self-care that downtime bestowed on you. You want some kind of special decompression chamber to ease the transition and prepare you, body and soul, for a return to the rigors of your regular life. Like the jet lag from flying east, it's hard switching from a non-ordinary time zone to the ordinary one.

Consider keeping one arm out of your self-made box and allow yourself to bring some of that playful, detached, refreshed, and renewed, expansive energy into your ordinary days. Who knows, you might turn your ordinary days into something extraordinary.

We either make ourselves miserable, or we make ourselves strong. The amount of work is the same.

Carlos Castaneda

Waiting

Waiting for important information is never easy. You know how it is. You are filled with anticipation. You keep looking at the clock. Your mind is a Tilt-A-Whirl of scenarios and possibilities. You don't know what's coming. Is the answer yes or no? Is the news good or bad? You have no idea. Your wait has emotional heft. It's hard to contain yourself, much less put your focus on something else.

However, in an effort to maintain control and feel productive, you try to distract yourself by making a call, getting a cup of coffee, or reading a magazine. It is difficult to concentrate. Everything in your being is geared toward the information you're expecting at any moment. You find yourself hypervigilant. You listen for sounds that might signal that what you're waiting for is at hand, be it the sound of footsteps, the turn of a doorknob, the ping of an incoming e-mail, the buzz of a text message, or the ring of the phone. You keep looking for some small sign that your wait is nearly over. Every fiber of your being is awake and alive and readied for whatever is to transpire. You have played out every possible outcome in your mind.

And still you wait. Time crawls. The tension is palpable. Your mind is dedicated to hearing the news and finding sweet release from your anxiety. Your body tightens, clenches, wiggles, or rocks in a pull toward equilibrium. Everything about you is readied for the long-overdue response.

Time has now become a determining factor in your thinking. Too much time might mean this; too little time could mean that. You find yourself becoming irritated. The waiting drains your energy.

You discover that waiting itself is a fiercely private matter. Even if others are involved in the waiting process with you, each person's waiting may be experienced differently. Some might liken it to Dante's layers of hell; stoics may simply find waiting an inevitable reality and take it in their stride. The defeatists are resigned to expect the worst possible outcome; they slump and sigh in passive knowing that life is always hard. The optimists are positive and hopeful; they create acceptable solutions for every contingency. The fighters look at everything as a personal challenge; they are convinced that sheer will can conquer all.

Then there are those who are fueled by the tension; they place themselves as best featured player in the drama of unknowing; they create havoc and uproar. Waiting is not easy for most of us humans.

The unknown is scary. It can be anything, good or bad or in-between. It speaks of the future; it can trigger the past. It can portend great change. Waiting is akin to hanging out in a hallway with multitudinous closed and locked doors. You are standing in the hall, and, as the song goes, they hear you knocking, but you can't come in—at least not yet. You feel at the mercy of the powers that be. You have little or no control of the process.

Waiting asks you to sit with the mystery, and that can be stressful. However, it does offer an opportunity to call upon your Best Self to teach you patience and acceptance.

Waiting can remind you that you are resilient; you have opened and reopened your heart more than you ever dreamed possible in love, compassion, and caring. Waiting reminds you that there are always options, some a little harder to swallow than others. Waiting reminds you that you are courageous and tenacious. Waiting reminds you that your power is not held in the unfolding of the mystery but in how you choose to handle, manage and respond to it. Waiting is a call to trust yourself, be with yourself, and support yourself as you allow the mystery to unfold.

May your next wait be long enough to remind you of who you are and short enough to keep you sane.

There is always one unexpected little moment in life when a door opens to let the future in.

Graham Greene

Procrastination

You have a project to do, a task to complete, or a deadline to meet. The target date looms ominously before you.

You know you have to get this project done; on some level you actually want to finish this undertaking. However, you seem to get in your own way. There is always something else to do—another chore, a snack to eat, someone to assist, an e-mail to answer, a box to empty, papers to sort, keys to find, errands to run, music to clear your head, a nap to revitalize you, anything but what you need to do.

When you find yourself in this all too familiar place, you may wonder why. You are feeling full of stress and unhappy with your non-performing, avoidant self. Why do you put off today what needs to be done by tomorrow—or even later today? You hate this about yourself. This tendency to procrastinate makes you feel awful. Others view you less than favorably as well.

Understanding your motivation may offer some insight and help you become more mindful. Here are some possibilities for you to consider.

Are you a perfectionist? Do you delay in an unconscious way in order to guarantee that your outcome will be less than stellar? By having no time to do the job well, you have effectively removed perfection from the mix.

Are you angry about the project or the people involved with this task? By avoiding the project, you have passively allowed your anger to surface.

Are you operating from a place where you have lost confidence in your abilities to accomplish and succeed? Has your self-worth taken a nosedive?

Are you feeling overwhelmed, uncertain, and unclear about the task at hand? Have you become paralyzed with fear, like a deer in the headlights?

Do you continually create these last-minute emergencies so you do not have to step into the fullness of who you are and accomplish what you really want to do in this lifetime? In other words, are you sabotaging yourself?

Do you have ADD tendencies that require screaming surges of adrenaline to meet any target date?

Do you have a tendency to create drama in order to be rescued and avoid taking responsibility?

With new insight about how you operate, it can be easier to look procrastination in the face. Procrastination, after all, is simply a maladaptive coping response.

The next time a deadline looms, give yourself some time to strategize the best way of meeting the challenge. You might need to plan ahead, ask for help, request clarity, create small steps, believe in yourself, get in touch with your feelings, or banish negative self-talk. Understanding how you work and identifying your personal subtext goes a long way toward getting the procrastination monkey off your back.

One must still have chaos
in oneself to be able to
give birth to a dancing star.
Friedrich Nietzsche

The enchanted forest of puzzlement

PART 1: A STORY

Once upon a time, a traveler walked down a well-marked path. The more the traveler walked, the more confident she became. She felt more and more empowered with each purposeful stride.

On this particular day, the air temperature was just right, the sky was that expansive, everything-is-possible blue, and there were clouds—loads and loads of white, puffy clouds sailing around the nimbus of the earth.

It was a perfect, happy day. The traveler whistled as she moved ahead. She had a glint in her eye, determination on her belt. Her pockets were full of certainty and bravado. The world was hers. Everything was in sync, everything was going well. She was making excellent progress.

Until she took a small stumble that ended in a big rumble as she rolled down the bank of the path.

The traveler's fall stopped abruptly as she found herself knee-deep in leaves, twigs, and confusion. She was disoriented. She had no idea what had happened, much less where she was. She was completely lost. The traveler realized she was assuredly off-road and, most certainly, off the beaten path.

The traveler staggered to her feet and looked for some sign that could direct her back to the familiar trail. Sadly, there was no such marker. The traveler became angry; she tightened her belt and looked for other ways to solve her dilemma. The more she looked, the angrier she became. Her backpack of resources provided no solace. She wanted answers, solutions, and guarantees—and she wanted them now. She was wild-eyed with worry and projections, and all she could hear was the damnable hooting of some early night owls.

Alas, there were no ready-made answers, solutions, or guarantees for the traveler. Her peregrination had taken a seemingly wrong turn.

Unbeknownst to the traveler, there were no owls in this woodland; there were only three witches hooting to each other in the treetops. The witches, Bemused, Bewildered, and Baffled, were doubled over with laughter at the hilarious antics of the traveler trying to find her way out.

It was like a child playing cat's cradle with yarn; the more she tried, the more stuck she became. The traveler's multitudinous efforts created a force field, like laser light security at a museum, so that she was locked deeper and deeper within the confines of the forest. There was no way out: the traveler had unknowingly rolled right into a charmed forest.

To be exact, the traveler was being held captive in the Enchanted Forest of Puzzlement. In this forest, perplexity and mystification reigned. It was a no-win situation if one did not know the key to being freed from the enchanted puzzlement.

The traveler tried and tried, but every action closed the forest further in around her. She was losing ground at an alarmingly speedy rate, and she was becoming more and more panicked. And the more she panicked, the more the forest shrunk itself around her. Before she knew it, she had only a small plot of forest floor to call her own. The far reaches of the forest were impossible to negotiate. The traveler was locked in a leafy green hell.

Eventually the traveler became so very weary and so tired from all her efforts that she finally gave up her struggle and made a nest of pine needles and moss, where she stretched out and let herself fall into a state of deep, deep sleep. She no longer heard the hooting of the witches. Her mind quieted, and her body rested.

And as she slept, she dreamt of floating in moonlight, through a green, green forest, where the treetops held sleeping witches, and coming upon a bridge.

When the traveler awoke from her dream, the moon was full and the forest was still. The traveler knew now just what to do. She rolled over and went back to sleep looking to finish her dream.

PART 2: THE MORAL OF THE STORY

Puzzlement holds a tremendous magic. It is difficult to free ourselves from confusion and worry. Certainty is comforting. Yet the spiritual path, as we well know, is anything but linear. There are always surprises, changes of venues, unexpected guests, unusual circumstances, and the occasional witch or two.

To break the powerful pull of puzzlement, we need to stop moving. It is important to become very, very still. The body and mind need rest. The soul calls for quiet so that its wisdom can surface and we can find our way. The soul provides markers, be they dreams, meditation, or that quiet little voice that whispers in your ear. We have the answers. We just get confused and sometimes think everyone else knows better. Truth be told, if we just hunker down for long enough and listen with an open, loving heart, the answer is always there.

As the indigenous elders always advised, when you are in doubt, take no action. I agree and will amend that thought with the following: When you find yourself held captive in the Enchanted Forest of Puzzlement, surrender to the greenery, rest, and wait for your soul to give you the answer. You'll be on your way before you know it.

*To climb steep hills
requires slow pace at first.*
William Shakespeare

Resistance

You feel somewhat like an ant that is trying to climb up a steep hill carrying an enormous crumb securely fastened to its back. Like the ant, you, too, are carrying what feels like a huge burden. A project you gladly took on and expected to complete with relative ease has become an incredibly taxing endeavor.

Alas, despite your good intentions, you find yourself dispirited and unfocused. You find every reason imaginable not to attend to your task. You become distracted with other activities. You are tired, hungry, and wanting to do anything but the project at hand. You feel miserable. You are whiny. You are angry that you cannot get into the groove and efficiently meet your goal. You have lost that productive edge. You think it's such a nice day, you'd rather have some fun.

Then you remember, your project is not duty; you volunteered for it. You raised your hand and said, "Yes, I want to do this. I can do this. This challenge excites me." This is what you chose; this is what inspired you. You then wonder, Why am I having such a difficult time doing what it is that I said I wanted to do? This doesn't make sense. Why am I stuck when I want to go forward?

The gods of wonder hear your query. They ask you to hold on a bit and hang out in the push-pull of your feelings. They realize it's mighty uncomfortable but assure you that these feelings are time-limited. Feel the push-pull, they counsel. Your situation will find resolution in the not-so-distant future if you are willing to listen to the faintest of small voices trying to get your attention.

Perhaps you are, on an unconscious, out-of-your-awareness level, afraid. This is most likely a very old fear or combination of fears, born out of beliefs, experience, acculturation, and conditioning. There are any number of fears, but the most likely culprits are the fear of success and the fear of failure. These twin fears are a tag team of push-pull. You are afraid to go up and you are terrified to come down. What will be expected of you? Will you be abandoned? Will the crowd throw tomatoes at your head?

Someone wise once said that what you resist, you already own. Resistance tells you that you have begun. There has been some sublevel agreement, some acqui-escence to the project at hand. You have already agreed to participate. You have made the investment; there has been an exchange of thoughts, emotions, and energy.

Resistance is like a waterwheel in that it never stops rotating. Resistance provides you with a barrier of protection so that you do not rush fully into the raging waters. You keep plodding along, one minute forward, another minute back. The constant grind fine-tunes your focus, again and again. The chronic revolving motion calls for you to commit and recommit, over and over.

Like the hammering of metal into a blade point, resistance hones your process. It takes your energies, willingness, talents, doubts, fears, attention, and intentions and sharpens all these elements into an edge of force. Now you focus totally and you are ready to complete your mission. You have everything you need; it has all coalesced within you. You go forward.

Resistance is a necessary component of the challenge cycle, and, as such, consistently and consciously overcoming resistance leads ultimately to success.

*Be joyous, even though
you have considered all the facts.*
Wendell Berry

Escape

When we get out of the glass
bottles of our ego,
and when we escape like squirrels
turning in the cages
of our personality
and get into the forests again,
we shall shiver with cold and fright,
but things will happen to us
so that we don't know ourselves.
Cool, unlying life will rush in,
and passion will make our bodies taut
with power,
and old things will fall down,
we shall laugh, and institutions will
curl up like burnt paper.

D. H. Lawrence

Flight grounded

You have been climbing up this staircase, pursuing your intention, every day. All too often it seems long—very long. Never ending, in fact. Sometimes you think reaching the top seems impossible. When does it end? Why does this ongoing push, day after day, seem so difficult and exhausting? Yet you seem riveted to your pursuit. It is part of you; you are part of it. It cannot be ignored or dismissed. Turning back never seems like an option. So you continue, even when each step feels heavy and burdensome.

But sometimes you get stuck on the landing. You put one foot on the next step and nothing happens. You can't go any farther. You're stalled. There is no movement; your feet are wearing shoes of stone. You are stuck on the landing between flights.

Your flight has been grounded. The landing feels confining; there is no progress, no motion. You feel as though there is no air; you are having difficulty breathing. What's the hold-up? Why this inactivity? Who instigated this inertia? You are stymied and perplexed.

Your mind is like a whirling dervish. You have moved into panic. You beseech the gods, *Tell me what's going on!*

And the gods do not answer, at least not immediately.

When nothing is certain—
everything is possible.

Margaret Atwood

Houston, we have lift-off

There you are, churning and spinning. Your hands are sweaty, your shoulders are knotted, your jaw is clenched, and your stomach is crummy. Your sleep has been restless. You have been preoccupied and have had a tendency to stare into space. You are not on your game. Life stinks right now. You are held hostage on the landing, between flights, with nowhere to go. The gods have been less than helpful. You are supremely cranky.

Then, seemingly out of nowhere, there is a shift in the atmosphere. It becomes easier to breathe, you can stretch your legs, and your mind is no longer attached to a carnival ride. A small insight taps your shoulder. You lean down and extend an ear. You understand that you have been afraid.

Who, me? Afraid? Yes, your insight alerts you to that small, dark, unconscious part of yourself, the part of you that has been holed up in a back corner. You realize you were not aware of the fear—until now. Now you are ready to pull that scaredy-cat fear out from the tight spot, bring it into the light of day, nourish it with some milk, and understand that it is a very, very, very old fear. Once seen in the light and fed some nourishment, you can let this ancient scaredy-cat go. There is no more fear.

With the fear released, you notice that your feet are feeling light and bouncy. While insight talked with you, the gods outfitted you with new shoes. They look sleek, sturdy, and capable of letting you take the stairs two at a time. Clearly, you are ready to zoom up the next flight.

Fear is the cheapest room in the house. I would like to see you living in better conditions.

Khwajeh Shams al-Din Muhammed
Hafez-e Shirazi

Monkey Minds
and Tender Hearts

"No, no, that's not a sin, either. My goodness, you must have worried yourself to death."

Pop! goes attention

It's not easy being a free-floating entity in a jam-packed cosmos that competes for one of your most precious resources, your attention.

Attention is a matter of personal choice. We often forget that we have choice, and choice is the ultimate in personal power. Every day we regularly get to choose where we will invest our energy and our time and how we will fill our senses.

The world is chockablock with stimulus overload. We choose almost everything that fills and influences our day: entertainment, food, sports, websites, people, places, and things. We choose where to direct our attention, how to spend our time, and where to spend our money.

Attention is a choice, and it is our first choice. This makes attention a form of power.

Shamans have been teaching the concept of attention as power or energy for centuries. Whether you call it chi, qi, or prana, energy is our life force. Attention is how we choose to direct that energy.

Harvard University's Dr. Herbert Benson and his team studied Tibetan monks who were able to maintain their body temperature while meditating in freezing temperatures outside. Shrouded in cold, wet sheets, the monks' meditation practices dried the sheets from their body heat. Talk about the power of attention.

Amazingly, with practice, we all have this inherent power to direct our lives by consciously and mindfully choosing where to place our attention and to maintain our focus. We have the built-in hardware to be more of a powerhouse than we ever imagined.

Each of us literally chooses, by way of his attending to things, what sort of universe he shall appear to himself to inhabit.

William James

The flow of focus

It's sometimes so hard to maintain our focus. The world is full of so many delicious distractions. It almost seems easier to be preoccupied. Focus requires commitment and dedication. Focus demands our complete, unadulterated attention. Sustained focus is an act of will that delivers us into a channel of flow.

Focus moves us from the corners and edges where we are hanging out, having coffee, chatting up friends, running more errands, reading e-mail, and the like. Focus calls us to the core, no more dillydallying, no more busywork. Focus tells us it is time to go front and center. It is time to show up and be present.

That's the hard part. Focus doesn't want excuses or equivocations. There are no hall passes or incompletes with focus. You can't hide. Focus wants you in the spotlight, 100 percent in the now, body relaxed and ready, mind attuned and concentrating fully on the matter at hand. Focus doesn't fool around.

Focus is the bright light that connects us to flow— the flow of our thoughts and actions through which we meet the challenges a given task presents. Flow becomes the channel for focus. As the word implies, flow enables tasks to be completed almost effortlessly. It enhances your creativity. Flow is optimal focus.

Pursue some path, however narrow and crooked, in which you can walk with love and reverence.

Henry David Thoreau

Anchor points

What holds you? What keeps you grounded and tethered?

In today's world, there is much fast-paced changeability. Life seems to turn on a dime. Weeks vary; every day has a unique twist. As you routinely deal with the changes, variances, alterations, and reschedulings, what allows you to stay centered? How do you remain true to yourself?

If you do not have anchor points securely affixed to your routine, it is easier to lose your balance. There is nothing to ensure that you are grounded; you can easily be knocked off your center. Nothing is holding you or rooting you to your Best Self.

Anchor points provide those roots. They are regular routines that have become fully incorporated into your life. They are subjective by definition: What works for you may not work for me. Anchor points are anything that serves to balance and stabilize you. There can be the weekly phone call with a loved one, early morning walks with your neighbor, a class at the gym, reading before bed, keeping a journal, daily meditation, or prayer.

Anchor points reduce stress by providing a regular outlet by which you can physically, emotionally, mentally, or spiritually express yourself. They become fixed points of stability; they provide safety and security. When your life is totally upside down or you feel as if you are trudging through the desert with little hope of reaching the oasis, anchor points can help keep you sane. They anchor you in the here and now and deepen your connection with yourself.

Today, identify your anchor points and recommit to incorporating these grounding actions into your routine. To start, consider one anchor point commitment for 10 to 15 minutes a day—that's it. This daily action can make a huge difference.

If this idea inspires you, you might consider extending your commitment to yourself and try this for 21 days—the time is takes to create a new habit. Not only will you feel better, you will also have strengthened your self-esteem and self-confidence.

Practice is a seedbed of miracles.

Michael Murphy

Resentments

Have you ever felt supreme resentment over another's action? How dare they do that to you, you of all people? You have always been there for them. You have sacrificed for them. You have rearranged your life for them. They have the unmitigated gall to ignore, hurt, or rebuff you. *How could they?*

Sound familiar? Such is the human condition when you feel resentful. More than likely you have been insulted or betrayed. You feel they only thought of themselves. You were not considered in the mix. It's a painful place to be.

Resentments can be enormous and searing; they also can be subtle little wounds that continuously dig into your ego. Your feelings are hurt. You may share your affronted feelings with others in an effort to be validated and proven right, or you may silently nurse them.

Interestingly, resentments come bearing a message. It's as if the grand hall of your psyche has been opened with pomp and circumstance; the enormous trumpets are raised and sounded to herald the forthcoming proclamation. The communiqué is this: Resentments are signals that you are not being responsible for yourself.

"Not responsible," you sputter. "I am *always* responsible." Perhaps you are always responsible for and toward others. But the rub is, are you responsible for yourself? Have you stated your case, set your limits, created your boundaries, or contained your energies? Has there been a subcontext or a hidden agenda? Did you just give all of yourself away—again?

Resentments are potent reminders that you have not taken full responsibility for yourself, your needs, and your desires. Resentments have a hidden message—*Stand up for yourself*—that has yet to be identified, honored, or expressed.

Our resentments bind us to the person with a cord stronger than steel.

Emmet Fox

An emotional hangover

Ever have one of those weeks when there is palpable, anger-inciting tension between you and a family member? Or when you have had a crushing misunderstanding with one of your dearest friends? Or when an incident at work has you mumbling obscenities under your breath and double-checking your pension benefits?

As a result of some emotionally incendiary experience in which you feel wronged, not valued, misunderstood, or crossed, you can often find yourself on one wild ride of emotions.

Your feelings can spike to new highs. You can feel turbocharged with fury. You feel the blood coursing through your veins and throbbing at your temple. You are vibrating with anger, injustice, and hurt at the maddening insensitivity, sheer stupidity, or blatant passivity that has been bestowed on you. *How could they?*

And before you know it, you are off again on the careening roller coaster of painful feelings—up and down, swinging widely to the left, twisting up, crisscrossing to the right and zigzagging to a final lurching stop. You start talking about it again, and off you go, up, up, and away in a fiery fury. *How could they?*

You spin round and round until eventually you are spent. There is no more; simply the crumbling, white-ash embers of a fire gone dead. You are exhausted, drained, and totally depleted by the emotional highs and lows of your charged days. You have no energy. You feel like a truck has used your body for parallel parking practice. You are a pulverized mass of once-quivering emotions. You have an emotional hangover.

There is no hair of this dog for the morning after. There is no specialized rehab. Copious amounts of water to hydrate your burned-out system are of little avail. What's a suffering fool to do?

As with any good recovery effort, you need to acknowledge that you have a problem. Yep, this is your problem. "But *they* did it to *me,*" you howl. And so they did, but you, and only you, are responsible for your reactions.

Remember the Boy Scouts and their motto, "Be prepared"? That's good advice for preventing more of these emotional upsets. Whether you stirred the pot or someone else came after you with a figurative cleaver, there is value in understanding the dynamics of challenging confrontations. Without awareness, the emotional set-to simply dissolves into yet another debilitating incident of high drama.

Let's consider a few possibilities for circumnavigating the next big tumult:

ARE YOU TOO EMOTIONALLY ATTACHED TO
THE OUTCOME OF THE INTERACTION? DO YOU
HAVE TO WIN? DO YOU NEED TO BE RIGHT?

You know the expression: Would you rather be right, or would you rather be happy? I can say, and I believe, that being right is overrated, but, boy, howdy, when I feel I am right, that's Right with a capital R, it is very hard to let go and consider another viewpoint. It takes some emotional maturity to get off that high horse and to find common ground.

IS THE EMOTIONAL EVENT THE RESULT OF A
POWER STRUGGLE, A NEED FOR CONTROL?

There is a saying among sales reps: The one who cares the least has the most power. In other words, when you are emotionally detached, you are better able to see the big picture, be open to alternatives, and respond with reason.

DID YOU CREATE DECENT BOUNDARIES AND CLEAR PARAMETERS SO THAT YOU PROTECTED YOURSELF?

A hallmark of high self-esteem is the ability to be assertive. It is not always easy, but it is clearly important. Further, one of the skills of effective communication is the ability to state your needs clearly. Are you able to ask for what you need and say no without feeling guilty?

ARE YOU AWARE OF WHAT BUTTONS ARE BEING PUSHED?

There is that old therapy joke about the patient telling the psychiatrist that his mother is pushing all of his buttons. The psychiatrist responds, "Of course she is. She installed them."

Seriously, though, be it family, friends, or astute observers of the human psyche, most of us can detect the soft, squishy places in one another. We are all more alike than we acknowledge. We want to feel respected and acknowledged, heard and valued. But when buttons are being pushed—and they are usually pushed to get a reaction—we can feel rejected, shamed, guilty, unworthy, and all manner of not good enough.

When we are aware of our hot buttons, we can be better prepared; we can respond instead of react.

Are you willing to walk away, say no, and choose not to engage in the tension?

There is always choice. Choice serves as the grace note to every interaction. You can choose not to struggle, not fight, see it another way, speak your truth, state your case, agree to disagree, and so forth. There is a certain elegance in being able to disengage from drama and choose not to play the game.

Like most experiences in life, emotional hangovers can serve as good teachers. You can learn how to protect yourself for future interactions. You can train yourself to move away from the victim place by following the three A's: you can change your *action*; you can change your *attitude*; or you can learn to *accept*.

Automatically you have empowered yourself. Isn't that far better than having an emotional hangover?

When you blame others, you give up your power to change.

Robert Anthony

Be kinder than necessary,
for everyone you
meet is fighting some
kind of battle.

Plato (tweaked)

You've got to have heart

On the left side of your body, behind your ribs, there lies a wonder. It is your heart—courser of blood, animator of the body, maintainer of rhythms, keeper of memories, font of courage, home of compassion, place of mercy, safehold of love. This is your wondrous, ever-faithful heart.

Your heart beats with the true-bluest of your dreams, desires, and intentions. Your heart often knows before your mind does what it is that you really want and how you really feel. Your heart is wise; it holds memory—cellular memory—of all that you are, all that you were, and all that you can be.

When you are in alignment with your heart, there is no judgment, no bias, no blame, and no conflict, because the heart sees the oneness of all. And this brings peace into your life.

When you allow your heart to open and unfold, you find well-being, joy, and delight.

When you honor the strength of your heart, you are invincible.

When you are in sync with your heart, you are rooted into your very being and you are in balance.

When you listen to your heart, your intuition surfaces and you discover wisdom.

Today, allow your heart to lead the way.

Just trust yourself;
then you will know how to live.

Johann Wolfgang von Goethe

Blowing in the wind

Have you ever looked up into the corner of a window and seen a spider's web holding a leaf? It seems improbable that the web, with its fine, almost invisible threads, could hold the weightier leaf so securely, but it does.

We are often like that leaf, dropped from the mother tree and blown freely on various currents until we find ourselves attached to a web with little understanding of how or why we got there. The web holds us steady, even as our leafy self twists and turns in the breezes.

What the ancients knew, and what we are just discovering within the realm of quantum physics, is that everything is connected. Everything—every person, animal, plant, rock, lake—everything is energetically connected. We are connected by the energy of light; we are all held in a web of light that radiates love.

At those times when you feel buffeted by the winds of fate and find yourself disconnected and despairing, consider increasing your light on the Big

Web through the power of unconditional love. That's right. You can increase your amperage and bandwidth by loving yourself, your family, your friends, and your neighbors unconditionally. Unconditional love has no qualifications, no admissions tests, no criteria for acceptance. It is simply love that accepts unequivocally.

Radiate more light by loving someone unconditionally today.

The heart that breaks open can contain the whole universe.

Joanna Macy

He told me that once
he forgot himself & his
heart opened up like a
door with a loose hatch
& everything fell out &
he tried for days to put
it all back in the proper
order, but finally he
gave up & left it there
in a pile & loved
everything equally.

Brian Andreas, StoryPeople

Hardwired for connection

We cannot escape relationships. They are everywhere. They are the connective tissue of life. Friend, spouse, child, sibling, coworker, or neighbor, life is filled with relationships of varying dimensions, spheres of influence, and intensity.

Each of us is the product of some kind of connection. In fact, we are born into Relationship 101, a.k.a. our family, which serves as our first social unit and school for our first lessons in interpersonal dynamics. This is where personality styles are formed and family roles are acquired.

These early years are, indeed, formative. We develop our modus operandi of how we relate to others and how we operate in the world. Do we become bullies, pleasers, shrinking violets, peacemakers, or devil's advocates?

As life progresses, we advance through the relationship ranks. We learn how to make friends, create enemies, find love, taste passion, explore intimacy, plumb depths, fail love, and, if we are lucky, as well as courageous, refind love.

Relationships stretch us like a rubber band, sometimes to the point of breaking; they hollow us until our innards echo. They take us to the very edge and then call us back again.

Relationships test us. They make us question, cry, rant, rave, disavow, and betray; they also warm our hearts, make us glad to be alive, and allow us to jump for joy, smile incandescently, and howl with delight.

Relationships are good teachers.

Being deeply loved by someone gives you strength, while loving someone deeply gives you courage.

Lao Tzu

Tender shepherd

Think of the shepherd tending a flock, gently herding the sheep to greener pastures and guiding them to safety in a storm.

How might you require gentle guidance and tender shepherding? When might you need nourishment and a temporary space for rest and recovery—your own safe harbor, so to speak.

In a single day you are required to wear many hats: planner, doer, negotiator, peacemaker, strategist, cheerleader, manager, chauffeur, action hero, consumer, family member, employee, student, volunteer. It can be hard to manage your internal brood; it becomes a bit of a juggling act. Multiple aspects of you are required to act and respond appropriately to the demands of many situations and the concomitant roles you play. Deftly switching hats and changing roles throughout the day can be tiresome as well as stressful. Everyone wants a piece of you; your time and energy are at a premium. This takes a toll; you can feel as if there is no space in which to breathe.

How well do you nurture yourself? How often do you succeed in getting your own needs met? Are you too busy and other-directed to create time to rest, nourish your body, or feed your mind? Have you managed some fresh air and blue skies recently?

You do so much for others. It's important that you do for yourself as well.

Today, try a little tenderness.

The trouble with superheroes is what to do between phone booths.

Ken Kesey

Peel carrots, chop onions

It's the day-to-day faithfulness to yourself, your values, your family, and your work that gives continuity, substance, and foundation to your life. Without this sustained commitment, the steadying routine of life gets lost. There are no anchor points to ground the day.

It's important to remind yourself that even your most mundane daily tasks, performed consistently, are essential acts of fidelity. They serve as connective tissue. They help keep you, your family, community, office, school, and other assorted circles on an even keel. Your steadfastness, commitment, and ability to do as promised create trust.

You do what needs to be done, day in and day out. Everyday tasks come to be expected, and the regularity of your daily acts dilutes the significance of your actions.

Nonetheless, your day-to-day faithfulness serves as a gift of enormous dedication, care, and loyalty. Your daily acts foster connection, care, cohesion, and commitment. They provide the comfort of routine and everyday ritual; they nurture peace of mind. The sum of your actions is greater than you realize:

> You become the touchstone; you provide safety and security.

> You are the ballast; you tender the steadying influence.

> You are the beacon; you shine the light to refind home.

Take a minute to acknowledge your daily acts of faithfulness, and allow yourself to appreciate the difference you make.

The purpose of life is to increase the warm heart. Think of other people. Serve other people sincerely. No cheating …

The Dalai Lama

Balance

Balance is often elusive. Many of us say, "Yes, please, bring on the balance." We think of balance as a temporary resting place before we venture forth into more frenetic activity. But that is inaccurate.

Balance is an active state; there is nothing passive about it. Balance requires a fair amount of tenacity and grit—especially when events around us are challenging or even chaotic. It is not for the faint of heart. Balance demands focus. And here's the real rub: Balance demands an openness of the heart. It is impossible to maintain equilibrium if we are tightly constricted and knotted up like a pretzel.

Balance suggests a stable point amid other strong and often competing and compelling forces. Balance is about holding our own and not falling down or keeling over; we are standing with flexed knees and are able to take deep breaths. Balance keeps us upright.

Think of how a tightrope walker holds out his hands to stay balanced. We, too, need to metaphorically hold our arms wide open to maintain balance. This prevents us from tensing up and taking manic, tight-fingered control. What's more, by remaining open, we surrender and trust our ability to recover our balance should we slip or become unfocused.

We would all agree that it takes persistence and resolve to maintain our footing and stay centered. A yoga teacher once told me that to maintain balance and keep from falling over, you need to keep your eyes trained on one fixed point. Makes sense, doesn't it?

I suggest that the fixed point is actually deep within us. It is our connection with Source and our relationship with our Best Self, the wonderfully soulful part of us that has an expanded heart and detached vision.

Life is a series of events that continually test our ability to maintain balance. Experience after experience, time after time, we are confronted with situations that pluck and pull at our very being. There can be anger, doubt, fear, rage, despair, and grief. Yet we eventually discover that when we let go, open ourselves up, and reconnect with our divine aspect, we are able to regain our balance.

Perhaps it is time to call forth your Inner Tightrope Walker and allow yourself to remember your own ability to stay upright and be centered. All you have to do is open your arms and heart wide and stay focused on higher ground.

Be tough in the way a blade of grass is: rooted, willing to lean and at peace with what is around it.

Natalie Goldberg

Easy Does It

"Not guilty, because puppies do these things."

What do you see?

Do you see ...

        ... yourself hunched endlessly over your computer? Lists of countless tasks? Your calendar double- and triple-booked? Bathroom breaks as problematic? Working more and more and getting less and less accomplished because you are always in meetings?

Do you see yourself ...

        ... becoming short-tempered? Chronically multitasking? Having difficulty concentrating? Sleeping poorly? Eating on the run? Spending too much time in your head—thinking, strategizing, or worrying? Gulping caffeine? Working nights and weekends as a matter of course?

Do you see ...

        ... how harsh you are with yourself? The unrelenting standards you apply to your actions? That you are running on empty? Your inability to say no or set limits? That you have lost yourself? Are overtired? Out of balance?

Take a good look. Do you see …

… that you want to stop? That you do enough? That you are able to let go and create boundaries? Your whole self? The worth of your being?

Intelligence is quickness in seeing things as they are.

George Santayana

You are goodness and mercy and compassion and understanding. You are peace and joy and light. You are forgiveness and patience, strength and courage, a helper in time of need, a comforter in time of sorrow, a healer in time of injury, a teacher in time of confusion. You are the deepest wisdom and the highest truth; the greatest peace and the grandest love. You are these things. And in moments of your life you have known yourself as these things.

Neale Donald Walsch
Conversations with God: An Uncommon Dialogue

Crash, bang, boom

There is a day when you cross a threshold. You walk into another space of consciousness, a place where you decide you have had enough. No more. You are done. Finished. You cannot carry another burden, manage another effort, or create another strategy. You have reached a limit. Actually you have surpassed that limit and are at the place of no return. There will be no more strings of never-ending late nights, working weekends, on-call holidays, or last-minute travel.

You realize, with stunning clarity, that you alone are responsible for you. If you do not stop and execute some serious self-care, you are headed for a crash.

Crashing is not pretty. It forces you to attend to yourself. Your body might give out in some way and necessitate that you stop immediately and learn firsthand about self-care. Or you might find yourself overwhelmed mentally and overloaded emotionally, and your only possible response is a hasty retreat from the daily fray as you can no longer tolerate a single demand, query, or stressor. Further, your spirit may have grown weary, and you can be pushed to simply be, allowing silence and quietude to help heal your battered soul.

No matter how often family or friends rail at you to take your time and slow down, the choice is singularly yours to create different options and possibilities for yourself.

Before the *crash, bang, boom* happens, you can decide to cross the threshold into a less stressful life. With choice, you allow that there is another door for you to open or, at the very least, another way for you to open the door.

A man needs a little madness
or else he never dares to cut
the rope and be free.
Nikos Kazantzakis (Zorba the Greek)

If you do not change direction,
you may end up where
you are heading.
Lao Tzu

Perfectly human

You're so hard on yourself. You frequently belittle
and second-guess yourself. You didn't do this right.
You forgot to say that. You review prior conversations
and practice future ones in your head. You see every
gaffe, misstep, and wrong word as an unbearable
breach. You sometimes embarrass yourself with an
outburst or, even worse, silence. You hold yourself to
exceedingly high standards. You never measure up
to your expectations. You expect perfection; you get
humanness.

By definition, being human means that we are
fallible. We are also vulnerable. We are not impervious
to slings and shots. We are not made of steel and
concrete; we are magnificently flesh and bone, muscle
and tissue. We are sensate beings; we can see, taste,
hear, and touch the experiences of life. Our humanness
is our connective tissue; it's what connects you with
me. We are bonded by the experiential, the trial and
error, and the ups and downs of life.

Because being perfect leaves no room for error,

you can't make a mistake and learn from it. You can't earn wisdom from your experiences. Perfection does away with the smudges and shadows. There is no coloring outside the lines with perfection. Perfection calls for a definitive response; you are either perfect or you're not; there is no in-between. Perfection is linear, black-and-white, all-or-none. There is no wiggle room in perfect.

Mastery, however, offers a spectrum of possibilities. It breaks out of the confines of right or wrong, perfect or not perfect. Mastery invites you to try many different ways, build on miscalculations, missteps, and mistakes. Mastery breaks out of the two-dimensional box of perfection and opens possibilities for all sorts of new creations. Mastery invites your perfectly human self to come in and play with all the colors.

When you make the world tolerable
for yourself, you make the world
tolerable for others.

Anaïs Nin

Deep fatigue

Are you ready to acknowledge the deep level of fatigue that has settled into your body? You have run hither and thither; you have done this and that; you have been responsible and responsive. You have, on more than one occasion, overdrawn on your reserves. You have no more to give; there is nothing else you can do at this moment. You are bone weary. You are completely empty.

Allow yourself to surrender into the deep, deep level of fatigue that you are feeling. Give yourself permission to imagine that you are in a beautiful forest filled with sunlit greenery. There is a canopy of tree branches overhead that filters the soft light. The ground is covered with spongy pine needles. You can hear the call of the birds, the distant sound of a waterfall, the skittering of rabbits and squirrels as they tunnel under fallen leaves. You see yourself walking through this landscape. As you walk, you allow all your body's tension to slip away. With every exhalation, you let go of even more.

When you are ready, you find the perfect spot to stop and take in the scenery. As you settle yourself comfortably, you take this time to recognize how much you have been pushing yourself. Your Smarter Self knows better, but circumstances, history, and patterns have led you into a state of chronic busyness. This has allowed little room for reflection, much less time to grasp the personal cost of such nonstop demands.

Today, give yourself permission to rest.

The faster we go, the slower we need to be.
Peter Senge

If your compassion does not include yourself, it is not complete.
Buddha

The gods want you for a meeting

Today, the gods call you in for a meeting. They ask you to step beyond the dark velvet curtain and sit in the cosmic sunroom until they are ready for you. You willingly agree and are happy for the chance to rest in the light, however briefly.

As you wait, you begin to wonder why you have been chosen today. Are you in trouble? Are you getting a promotion? The longer you wait, the more your mind spins with wildly dramatic scenarios. You are now unquestionably nervous. You dread the meeting and can't wait for it to be over.

No sooner has that thought crossed your mind than the curtain opens and you are beckoned into the boardroom where there is an enormous conference table surrounded by the gods seated in thronelike chairs.

The atmosphere is somber; your anxiety is sky high. You are asked to be seated in your own thronelike chair, and the meeting is called to order. Today's topic: Why aren't you having more fun?

What?

Yes, the gods want to know why you are not having more fun. You have not even met your fun quota for the past few months. You are woefully behind in your numbers. It has become a matter of deep concern. You are working too hard, doing too much, and making everyone else happy, but you have forgotten yourself. They understand that you have commitments and responsibilities. Nonetheless, fun is a very important, relevant part of life. Fun operates from high-octane energy. Fun opens you to creativity. Fun relieves stress. Fun is in the here and now. Fun is connecting.

They, as a group, are very displeased that you have not honored yourself. To their way of thinking, this is not honoring them. Your mandate is to have more fun. Pronto!

You stammer and stutter. "Uh … exactly what do you mean by the word *fun*? Could you give me some examples?"

The gods are not amused. They thunder in response, *"You know what fun is!"*

You are incredulous at their very poor timing. Don't they realize how complicated your life is right now? You begin to whine, "I don't have the time. Really, I don't have the time. You just don't understand how busy I am. I have a major deadline this month. When could I do this? Next month, I promise, next month, or the one after that, when the weather is better, I will make sure I schedule some fun then. Plus, I don't have the money for real fun right now, so let's just put this on the back burner until next spring and we can talk about this matter of fun then. Just wait, I'll show you. Give me a little time and I will be on top of my numbers. I'll even be over my quota. What do you say? Can we talk in the spring?"

The gods respond with waves of silence.

And the silence electrifies the air, and you realize that you cannot talk your way out of this. You have learned the hard way that if you don't listen to the gods, they will go behind the scenes and rearrange the circumstances of your life. You have little choice but to heed their guidance.

OK, you get it. You bow your head in acquiescence. You have to immediately start including fun in your life. You wonder how you are going to make this happen with all the work and responsibilities before you. You trudge off, seriously wondering how you can have some fun.

And, now, Harry, let us step out into the night and pursue that flighty temptress, adventure.

Albus Dumbledore, in *Harry Potter and the Half-Blood Prince*, by J. K. Rowling

How we spend our days is how we spend our lives.

Annie Dillard

Just float

Ever have one of those days when you felt like you were just floating?

Imagine, if you will, that it is early morning and you have access to a small boat that you can easily navigate. The sky is blue and dotted with clouds; the air is crisp and clean. Best of all, it is very, very quiet. You see one or two fishermen on the distant horizon. Today, it's as if you have the lake to yourself. Everything looks freshly washed by the night breeze and uncovered by the first morning light.

You take yourself to a beautiful cove and drop anchor. You hear the water slapping against the hull of the boat and see the occasional fish poking through the mirrored surface of the water. You inhale blue and green, sun and fish. *Ahhhh* ... You breathe deeply and settle into the peacefulness around you. Your body slowly loosens the knots of tightness and tension. The everyday world seems far away. Your thoughts are nonexistent. You simply follow your eyes, eyes that rest on the shoreline where long reeds are softly swaying to and fro, to and fro in the water. The undulating rhythms and the warmth of the sun deepen your reverie. You settle into a deep state of relaxation and comfort.

And you simply float. Like a toy boat in a bathtub, you bob up and down with the smallest of swells. You don't have a care in the world. You are enjoying this very moment, this space and time. You have given yourself permission to relax. You are allowing yourself to restore your balance and refill your inner well.

Allow your imagination to take you to such a restful spot and take some time to refresh and renew; give yourself an opportunity to just float.

Go within or go without.

Unknown

Come sit

Come sit. Come sit by the babbling brook. Come sit under the coolness of the trees, where the sunlight is soft and diffuse and becomes green-gold.

Take a moment and allow yourself to rest in this tranquil place. The only sound is that of the burbles and gurgles from the brook. Everything serves to deepen your sense of release. Everything serves to take you deeper and deeper into a place of relaxation.

Breathe in the silence. Breathe in the greenness. Breathe in the cool, shaded waters and allow yourself to be refreshed and renewed by the comfort of this place.

With a moment just like this, you can create peace. Peace begins with small moments ...

... when you stop.

... when you allow your breath to lengthen.

... when you allow yourself to be held in stillness.

… when you drop into silence.

… when you release thought, expectation,
   or anticipation clouding your mind.

… when you rest in the rhythms of nature.

Peace begins moment by moment.

*Nature, time, and patience
are the three great physicians.*

Chinese proverb

Can you listen?

Can you hear the rustle of a curtain against an open window?

Can you hear the soft breaths of a child sleeping?

Can you hear the low rumble of thunder on the distant horizon?

Can you hear the contagious laughter of a friend?

Can you hear the sound of footsteps on a forest path?

Can you hear the hum of tires on a distant highway?

Can you hear the sounds of a snoozing dog?

Can you hear the throbbing sound of your refrigerator?

Can you hear the pealing sound of church bells?

Can you hear the water tumbling over rocks in a mountain stream?

Can you hear trees dancing in the wind?

Can you hear the sounds of children playing and dogs barking late on a summer evening?

Can you hear the morning songs of the birds?

Can you hear a house settling into night?

Can you hear the exuberance of winter fun on a nearby hill?

Can you hear your love singing?

Can you hear the tinkling of wind chimes swaying in the breeze?

Can you hear the flicker of a candle flame?

Can you hear your quiet voice that resides deep within?

Can you hear your heart's desires?

Can you hear the whisperings of your soul?

Knowledge is received only in those moments in which every judgment, every criticism coming from ourselves is silent.

Rudolf Steiner

Church bells

In the late afternoon, when the busyness of the day has worn down your focus and resolve, your mind begins to travel and starts putting down roots in the evening to come. Perhaps there is the promise of a meal, some companionship, a special night, or simply a chance to relax. Your attention has begun to shift, and you are rocked into a sense of reverie as you hear church bells ring the hour. The bells signal the day's end; evening has arrived. It is the time of twilight.

Twilight marks those betwixt-and-between hours separating day from night. It is a liminal time when the veil between the worlds is thinner. The light becomes dim and dusky, tinted with blues and purples. The evening energy pulses in suspended animation, suggesting that anything can happen at this cusp of the day.

You are vulnerable at these hours. Your circadian rhythms have dipped; your attention has flagged. You are in need of a boost. You are most likely fatigued or stressed and stretched by too many demands.

When you hear the chiming of the church bells or notice the evening hour on the clock, here is a suggestion:

Allow yourself to stop momentarily and take a few moments of quiet.

Realign your energy by taking some deep breaths, and stretch out the tightness in your body.

Center yourself with calming, positive thoughts.

Allow yourself to move into a more even-tempered and neutral space.

In this way you shift your physical self, your attitude, and your feelings and can create a soothing prelude to the night just ahead.

Sometimes the most important thing in a whole day is the rest we take between two deep breaths.

Etty Hillesum

A little night music

There is something about music played under the
evening sky of summer. The music is not contained
by walls or rooftop; people are not restrained by pew,
chair, or table. The rules have softened; decorum gives
way to delight. It becomes a time out of time, *kairos*
time, when magic is afoot.

Everyone within the spiral of sound is joined
together. All are included, even those outside the
perimeters of the music-making. There are sweet
smiles and enraptured faces on those who walk the
neighborhood, their heads tilted toward the seductive
sound, drawn like bees to a flower. Windows open
wider to take in the delightful surprise. Dogs and
cats are contentedly settled as they are lullabied
to sleep.

The melodies permeate the night air and travel
into opened windows where babies remember the
angels. The sounds cascade like musical rain on
nearby gardens where parents happily listen and hold
hands in their candlelit backyard.

As the evening deepens into night, dancing becomes effortless. Movement is spontaneous and rhythmic. Singing is communal. The music plays to the heavens, and the emerging stars twinkle in concert.

It's a night of sweet connection and happy moments. It's a night to remember.

Great truths are felt before they are expressed.

Pierre Teilhard de Chardin

Quiet answers

We often forget that deep within us reside the answers to our questions and concerns. We look for experts; we surf the Web; we read articles, papers, and books; we canvass our friends. Yet we rarely consider taking our own deep counsel. We assume there are others who know better.

Curiously, there is no one on this planet who knows you as well as you know yourself. You are the expert. You know what resonates with you. You know what calls for your attention. You know that quiet little voice that has often calmed your fears and directed your actions. And yet, you forget to listen, or you discount your own wisdom.

You fear that you are not absorbing an insight correctly, or you have misunderstood it. You think it's your ego talking, and now there are other facts to consider. It all comes to the fore: every doubt, every fear. You undervalue what you know. You have forgotten how to trust yourself. You have given your authority over to the other so-called experts.

However, with every moment you have an opportunity to begin anew. You can begin the process of reconnecting with yourself. You can begin to listen to or sense the quiet wisdom that is inherently part of your nature. That wisdom is always present. Begin to trust yourself and reconnect with your wisdom. You know what's right for you.

The next message you need
is always right where you are.

Ram Dass

Natural Rhythms

"And only you can hear this whistle?"

Silent white

As the snow falls, it muffles the sounds of traffic, blankets the colors of sidewalks and roofs, outlines bare tree limbs, and softens the entire landscape into a scene of wintry whiteness.

Snow brings squeals of delight to children who are ready to sled and sling snowballs—and holds near the promise of a school-free day. You, on the other hand, are likely to busy yourself with the practical considerations—checking on supplies of food, firewood, and winter wear, shoveling snow, and finding out whether the roads are safe enough for travel.

Before the tasks begin in earnest, allow yourself the moment in time to stand outside and behold a temporarily muted world and absorb the beauty of such a blanketed tableau. The hush and stillness of a good, deep snowfall is indeed a gift from the gods. You breathe in the cold, frosty air, watch the snowflakes tumble to your feet, and hold yourself close.

As you take it all in, you marvel at the momentary quiet that envelops you in suspended animation. There is little or no sound. It is almost surreal. You have found yourself at a literal still point, a rare luxury in your life. You surf the waves of stillness and enjoy the temporary calm. The silent reverie holds you. You feel realigned by the quiet.

There are no accidents whatsoever in the universe.

Ram Dass

Icicle magic

It's a winter's night. You are comfortably ensconced in the warmth of your bed. At some point in the middle of the night you surface momentarily from the depths of your sleep to recognize the ping of ice crystals against the windows. You mentally scan the house and know that all is secure, all are safe. You roll over, snuggle deeper under the covers, and slip into another cycle of sleep.

In the morning you awake to find yourself in the midst of breath-catching brilliance. Everything sparkles in the morning sun. The light bounces off every possible surface. The radiance is dazzling. Everything is encased in ice from the wide expanse of field and roof to the smallest details of pine needle, leaf, and branch. The ice crystallizes the landscape, and the sun brightens it still more with tiny rainbows of refracted light. Everything has become a prism. It is a sight to behold. It is all there before you to enjoy, simply by taking some time.

Yet how often do you stop to marvel at the gifts and rhythms of nature? Often in the daily rush the primary concern is besting Mother Nature so that work, school, and chores proceed in their usual get-it-done fashion. There is little time to stop, be present, and admire the beauty before you. You hastily note the magnificent light show as you race out the door. Your days are busy and more than full. The ice storm is yet another impediment for you to overcome. The modern world leaves little time for dalliance.

Interestingly, the Ancient Ones had a different perspective. They viewed such gifts from nature as opportunities for soul nourishment and healing—a chance to bask in its wonder and listen for its lessons.

Today, will you consider a little one-on-one time with Mother Nature?

Never lose a holy curiosity.

Albert Einstein

Cold warmth

There is something about the cold quiet of winter and the muted hush after a snowfall that seems to soften and slow the rhythms of nature. The landscape is at a standstill; all is held in snow and ice. Mornings bring hoary frosts. Afternoons hold the promise of a bright sun in clear, cold air. Purpled sunsets, quick to come, announce day's end and the lamplit comforts of home.

When cold enough, we seek warmth—the warmth of a crackling fire, a woodstove, or heat thanks to a turned-up thermostat. We also seek the warming comfort of hearty meals shared with others; the heavenly scent of freshly baked bread, simmering soups, and hot chocolate; the steaminess of a hot bath; the cozy pleasure of flannel sheets and fleecy pajamas; the toasty weight of a favorite quilt; and the excuse to cuddle a little longer.

The cold brings us indoors; the cold inspires us to reach out and to find the pleasures of connection and comfort. The cold teaches us that it is difficult to be both cold and alone. Coldness looks for warmth—from a loved one, from friends, or from creature comforts. Cold is heat-seeking.

Today, consider what warms up your chilly self.

*One kind word can
warm three winter months.*

Japanese proverb

Spring storms

Lightning flashes fiercely, thunder rumbles ominously, winds whip frenetically, and spring rain pours down in sheets. At this moment, you find yourself in the season of changeable weather systems, externally and internally.

As the ground releases the grip of deep freeze and the unsettled forces of Mother Nature swirl about in riotous glee, so may the human psyche ricochet about in conundrums of will and desire. Unconsciously, the body-mind may know that the season of change, rebirth, and renewal is weeks away; there are internal contractions as the body-mind prepares itself to change.

The beauty of the storms is that they not only prompt us to acknowledge the forces of nature, but they also, symbolically, move us out of our comfort zone. We no longer move about our days unconsciously; we now look to read the signs and portents of the heavens and winds.

What a gift! We are called to stop and pay

attention. The wind whirls away the outdated debris of our thoughts, the rains open and release all the stuck emotions, the thunder reminds us of our unacknowledged angers, and the lightning strikes at the heart of our misplaced power and effectiveness.

The turbulence changes the landscape; it creates havoc and upheaval that serve as the precursor of change. The stormy weather prepares the seedbed for growth.

Today, consider the deep influences of storms in your life.

We cannot find peace if we are afraid of the windstorms of life.

Elisabeth Kübler-Ross

Faded summer flowers

It's a summer evening. You have returned home from your busy day. You take a moment for yourself and step out into the small patch of garden that has given you so much delight, pleasure, and fulfillment over the summer. Literally, your garden has fed your soul with its colors and beauty. You have enjoyed many a breakfast with the garden as your companion.

It is with a bit of sadness that you take in all that the garden has offered. You notice petals that have faded into a stiff ivory with the sheerest pink blush; flowers that have dried whole and intact, their full bloom a testament to their grandeur; vines and stems that have shrunken and dropped; and the yellowed and browned leaves whose verdant lushness have gone.

There are flowers that bore witness to hours of summer fun and squeals of delight. They had danced happily in the garden and graced the kitchen table with sun-warmed bouquets. Now, they have tired of the relentlessness of summer heat; they have grown weary of the abundant flourishing and have gracefully faded into the palest imitation of their former vivacity.

And there are always a few bold ones that choose to linger and in their singularity bring a much appreciated kind of beauty. The late bloomers are always a surprise and, usually, a glory. They stand there amid the blooms now spent and charge the air with the tenacity and vibrancy of life. Their splendor is even more appreciated given their audacity to stand so beautifully among the dead and dormant.

Today, you smile. The garden still brings you joy. The faded summer flowers speak of tender summer memories, and the late bloomers always bring a burst of hope.

The earth laughs in flowers.
Ralph Waldo Emerson

Morning shower

Can you envisage it? It's a gray morning with the sky seemingly within reach. The densely pearled clouds are hanging low and the air is thick with moisture.

The showers come early in the day, revitalizing the garden. The leaves shimmer verdantly with renewed vigor, and flower petals sparkle with droplets of rain. Everything is misted; it all glistens—clean, fresh, new. It feels like a gift.

As the day unfolds, the sky and the garden, the rain and the greenery seem so close. It feels intimate and personal. It's as if the heavens have decided to drop their loftiness and, for just a few moments on this spring morning, have chosen to lightly touch the earth with a full embrace. The very air shimmers. You feel almost as if you are trespassing in a province that is not yours to claim. You feel the hand of the divine. This morning has taken the ordinary and blessed it.

Time has stopped with your awareness—allowing you to take in the experience of the beauty as well as the beauty of the experience. You have felt the embrace of the whole. Your day has shifted beyond the reflexive impulse that sends you rocking and racing into hours of activity. This morning shower has reminded you that you, too, are part of heaven and earth. You are connected. It has reaffirmed that this intimacy is a gift as well.

Are you ready to walk into the embrace and feel the connection?

Let yourself be drawn by the pull of what you really love.

Rumi

Spirals

The shape of the spiral is a gift of the universe; think of galaxies, shells, or the conical structure of lilac or wisteria flowers. The spiral form flows; it allows for contraction and expansion, rebirth, and evolution. A spiral can create dramatic change; think of the spinning tornado. Spirals look to blend disparate elements. Consider mixing two paint colors, stirring two ingredients into a recipe, or adding cream to coffee. Then there is the function of the screw; it is the spiral that incorporates two variables.

The spiral begins in small, tight loops that expand into wider arcs. It spins in perfect momentum, always maintaining its shape, never losing its balance.

So, too, are you like the spiral. You start out tight and compressed, and then life happens. There are growth spurts, experiences, developmental leaps, understanding, openings, and insights. You have maintained your essence, but your being has expanded in what it knows and what it has gleaned from experiencing life. The wider loops of life are the expansion of your awareness and consciousness.

Consider yourself a spiral of energy interacting with all the variable elements that cross your path. Think of yourself as spiraling into whatever comes your way. See yourself—your being—as a spiral opening into the world, always maintaining your balance and never losing your momentum. Whenever you find yourself overwhelmed, place yourself and your considerable energy into the flow of the spiral. Allow yourself to spin closely into safety or spin widely into tranquillity.

When I dare to be powerful—
to use my strength in the service
of my vision—then it
becomes less and less important
whether I am afraid.

Audre Lorde

Helpful Strategies

"What's the next best medicine?"

The alchemy of smiling

It's easy enough to do. No one teaches you how to smile. There are no courses that teach smiling. This behavior is built into our DNA. Babies are known to smile in the womb and in their infancy. These smiles are simply reflexive facial movements, but as early as six weeks of age babies smile consciously—at first usually in response to seeing a parent's face. Children generally smile freely and easily, with grins of delight and pleasure. Grown-ups, on the other hand, tend to be more reserved and less spontaneous about smiling. With their personas securely in place, adults may sometimes flash calculated smiles—to gain approval, to win favor, even to deceive.

Do you realize that smiling is catalytic? It can change your internal chemistry. Now for the smile to pack this kind of wallop, it needs to be an authentic, high-voltage kind of smile, not merely a halfhearted grin or a pinched, tight-mouthed grimace. You have to really feel the source of the smile within your being. You have to connect with the source of your happiness, pleasure, and delight. And you need to be present, in the now, to connect fully with that which causes your eyes to twinkle, the corners of your mouth to lift, and your lips to part—possibly setting the stage for a giggle, guffaw, or hearty laugh to add to your merriment.

Whatever life path you tread, smiling is an essential tool for your journey. Smiling increases the release of endorphins in your body, perks up your brain chemistry, and lifts your mood. Smiling also relaxes your body by releasing tension. These effects brighten your energy field and recharge your immune function. And smiling makes you more radiant and therefore more magnetic. You draw to yourself more positive possibilities. All in all, smiling is a no-lose proposition, so engage in some serious work in psychoneuroimmunology. Smile.

Laughter is carbonated holiness.
Anne Lamott

Got stress?

Do you have a monkey mind that has run amok? Is there lots of chatter ricocheting around your cranium? Is there so much clamor and conversation inside your head that it's standing room only? Like the deli counter, do you need to take a number to discern which inner voice has taken over the microphone?

It's hard being a mental being—all those woulda, coulda, shouldas, all that plotting and planning, dissecting agendas, and scouting out subtexts. We live in the past, crying over symbolic spilt milk. We live in the future, doubled over with anxiety at the possibility of the worst-case scenario or the great cosmic shoe dropping onto our head. We can often be our very own idiosyncratic version of Chicken Little crying, "The sky is falling! The sky is falling!" We are so busy looking backward and forward, we don't see the hole in front of us, and we get twisted up, knotted, and stressed.

Stress and stress-related illnesses are at an all-time high. C. Norman Shealy, M.D., Ph.D., founder of the American Holistic Medical Association and author of *90 Days to Self-Health,* defines stress as the "total physical, chemical, and emotional pressure you experience." In other words, everything counts as a potential stress factor, be it the food you eat, the air you breathe, the exercise you do or don't get, and your perception of reality.

As a psychologist, I am particularly drawn to that perception-of-reality bit, because this is where the light can get tricky.

Someone wise once said that reality is what we perceive. I believe that to be true. There are days when we are like ducks in the rain; all the water rolls off our back. No worries, no fears, all those raindrops just join the pond water, and, like the duck, I merely shake off my tail feathers and I'm good to go.

Then there are other days when I'm not anything like a duck happily skimming the surface of the water. On those other days, I can step into a huge puddle and my shoes and clothes get saturated, or my car battery acts fussy, or my umbrella has gone MIA, and I arrive at the big meeting drenched and dripping.

In psychology, there is a certain inventory measurement that asks patients to rank life events for the past two years, such as a move, a job change, the loss of a spouse, or financial worries. The rankings are weighted numerically. The result of this inventory is a stress assessment. Stress is cumulative and, for some, the two-year inventory of stress makes the book of Job look like a musical comedy.

Most of us don't need a stress assessment to tell us we're stressed. But we might need someone to remind us that we're very stressed. We go and go and go. We don't eat well; we are sleep deprived, and the job or the family or life-in-general seems to demand more and more of our time and energy. Faster and faster become the norm. We even forget to breathe and blink.

Stress is a given in today's fast-paced, over-achieving, information-overloaded, and increasingly technical world. We all have it; we all know it. So what are we to do?

Relax, right? Relaxation is the antidote to stress. Relaxation allows us to recalibrate, take a deep breath or two, and refind our feet.

We often forget to get grounded in our bodies when we are stressed. We are so busy running the tape in our heads that we dismiss the rest of our being. We are operating from the shoulders up; it's as if we have become truncated at the neck.

Some people can't eat when they're stressed; others eat compulsively and quickly to stuff the burgeoning feelings. Some cannot sit still; others cannot sleep. Some get so overwhelmed, they make napping an Olympic event.

Whether we are in constant movement or unable to take a step, when we leave our bodies, we choose on some level of consciousness or unconsciousness not to feel the deeper, truer feelings that exist beneath the surface of stress.

For your consideration, here are a few coping mechanisms to help you defuse your stress and refind your balance.

LAUGH OR CRY

Admittedly, this may sound very basic and simplistic, but please realize that both laughter and crying are two of the foremost stress relievers. They are like steam vents that allow release of bottled-up energy and emotions. Like Joni Mitchell says, "Laughing and crying, you know it's the same release." Maybe it's time to rent a good movie that will allow you to howl with delight or have a good cry.

STOP

Make yourself a priority. Stop the merry-go-round and consider what it is you actually need right now. Can you give yourself the 20 minutes or 2 hours or few days you need to decompress and recalibrate?

EXERCISE

As we all well know, exercise is a great stress reliever. In moving the body and raising the heart rate, we increase the feel-good neurotransmitters.

UPGRADE YOUR LIFESTYLE CHOICES

When we're stressed, our whole being needs more support. Often, we shortchange ourselves, and our good habits get waylaid with the urgency of a stressful situation. When we are emotionally vulnerable, we are also physically vulnerable. And when we are physically vulnerable, we are also emotionally vulnerable. It is beneficial to create a daily rhythm and a lifestyle plan that support you during your seasons of stress.

FUEL THE BODY

When we're stressed, the simple carbs taste great and can be comforting, but think about some decent protein and vegetables. If you have goodies, eat them after the meal; your blood sugar (read: energy levels and moods) will be better regulated than eating simple sugars as your primary food group.

CONSIDER SUPPLEMENT SUPPORT

Vitamin C and a vitamin B complex are known to combat the effects of stress. Fish oils help the brain and the nervous system. Perhaps you might want to add a few supplements to your breakfast or lunchtime routine.

GO TO BED BEFORE MIDNIGHT

This helps the rhythms of your adrenal glands (the seat of the flight-or-fight response) and the interplay of your endocrine system.

EXPRESS YOURSELF

Write in your journal; share feelings with a friend; talk to your dog. Do whatever it takes to make you comfortable and allow your suppressed feelings to surface. There is great benefit in airing out your worries, fears, and concerns.

PRACTICE RELAXATION

Dr. Shealy, along with Harvard mind-body researcher Dr. Herbert Benson, author of *The Relaxation Response,* believes heartily in the benefits of relaxation. Relaxation in this context is considered to be a conscious permitting of the mind and body to become still, whether through meditation, prayer, communing with nature, listening to beautiful music, or observing art.

Shealy reports that two 20-minute segments of relaxation a day will decrease your body's stress response 50 percent. Start with 5 to10 minutes twice a day, and notice what happens. It really does make a difference.

MEDITATE

M-m-meditate? Yes, it really is doable! The hardest part is showing up and giving yourself the quiet attention. There is a myriad of styles and forms—something for everyone: mindfulness, lovingkindness, Transcendental Meditation® or TM®, insight, guided meditation, walking meditation. Start with 5 to 10 minutes a day. It will help quiet your mind and body.

UNKINK YOUR BODY AND REBALANCE
YOUR ENERGY

Try massage, body work, acupuncture, energy work, or yoga to help rebalance your body's energy flow.

You will feel like a million bucks when you have finished the session.

I think God's going to come down and pull civilization over for speeding.

Steven Wright

Rest and laughter are the most spiritual and subversive acts of all.

Anne Lamott

Take a breath

Take in a breath. Allow yourself to stop for a moment and feel your presence. You have been working so hard to accomplish all that needs to be done for your life to function. Now, stop and take a breath—a deep inhalation—one breath that reconnects you with your awareness and your physical and emotional selves. It is hard when you have had to live so mentally.

Take another breath and come more fully into your body. Draw the breath down into your belly and allow yourself to sink into your body and simply be. There is nothing to do here. You simply need to breathe. Be conscious of your gentle breaths becoming deeper and deeper as you relax more and let go. Let go of the stresses and strains, let go of the worries and fears. Allow yourself to be.

Take a few more deep breaths; reoxygenate your body and brain. Focus your breath on any tight or tense muscles and allow the breath to ease any discomfort you might hold.

It is time to be gentle with you. Life can be quite

hard and demanding. Now is your time to be with yourself—just a few minutes, that's all. Simply rest in the quiet, comfortable companionship of your breath and reconnect. You more than deserve it.

The biggest human temptation
is to settle for too little.

Thomas Merton

Invite your demons to tea

This wonderful exercise is from the Buddhist tradition. Imagine this, if you will: You head to the special gourmet market, high-end bakery, and flower shop. You buy the most sumptuous of delicacies and the most extravagant arrangement of early spring flowers. Once home, you unearth your finest table linens, which you wash and iron to perfection. You polish your silver until it gleams. You reach into the recesses of your cabinets and carefully withdraw your most delicate porcelains. You wash them in hot, soapy water and dry them mindfully with a hand towel. You set your table with all of your finery, creating a beautiful and inviting tableau.

You shower and dress, specially preparing yourself for this very important occasion, an occasion that requires the very best of everything you have to offer. With one final look in the mirror, you know you are completely ready.

You walk to the very back of your home, where there is a large wooden door with a small grated opening. As you approach the door, you can already smell the putrid, offensive odors and hear the snarling, banging, spitting, and other off-putting noises. You are quite nervous. You take a very deep breath. You open a series of locks, swing open the heavy door and invite your demons to follow you into the dining room for a tea party.

You are expecting your table to be trashed. But you are surprised. Your oversized demons sit carefully on your small-to-them chairs and place napkins in their laps. They are delighted to be included. You have actual conversations; you feed them sweets. You meet some of your deepest fears in these hairiest, most foul-smelling creatures. Who knew? You begin to feel some compassion; there's an inkling of comprehension. With some understanding, they really aren't so slimy, awful, and loathsome after all.

This month, will you invite your demons for tea?

Enlightenment is not about imagining figures of light but of making the darkness conscious.

C. G. Jung

119

If there is one door in
the castle you have been
told not to go through, you
must. Otherwise you'll just
be rearranging furniture
in rooms you've already
been in.

Anne Lamott

Grounding

Get comfortably seated, making sure your spine is straight. Take in a few deep breaths and bring your awareness into your body. Focus on the path of your breaths. Notice that with each inhalation and exhalation, your breathing becomes more relaxed, and your breaths easily grow deeper.

If your mind wanders, gently refocus on your breath. If your body posture is uncomfortable, take time to reposition yourself. It is important that you feel relaxed and comfortable. If you haven't done so already, close your eyes or allow them to become soft, without a particular focus, and continue to breathe.

Now invoke your active imagination to see, sense, or recognize the red, molten core of the earth. Imagine that you are pulling a translucent (light is able to shine through) red cord from the center of the earth. Simply invoke your active imagination and see, sense, feel, or know the red, molten core of the earth. In whatever way your imagination works for you, sense that with each in-breath, you are breathing the red cord up through layers (think gas, water, oil, rock, shale, limestone, etc.) of the earth until it loops through your tailbone. Then, with each exhalation, envision the cord descending down into the center of the earth again.

Now, powered by your breath, the red cord moves like a bicycle chain, each inhalation pulling up from the earth and each exhalation sending it back into the earth. Your breath is creating a cycle of connection, a circle of grounding. Take a few minutes to strengthen this connection with your breath and your intention. Allow yourself to feel connected to the earth and let your imagination guide you. There is no right or wrong. This is simply one method of grounding.

If you are grounded, if you have deep roots, then you, like a tree, can bend and sway with the elements. It's a helpful technique for connecting with your body and re-establishing balance.

Keep your feet on the ground
and your thoughts at lofty heights.
The Peace Pilgrim

Running energy

Running energy is a metaphysical practice to help you connect, align, and open your energy field. It serves as a beginning step that allows you to tap into the imaginal realm, access intuition, or move into a place of expanded awareness.

It's fairly simple and requires only your intention, attention, and focus. Here are the steps:

1. Visualize the molten, red core of the earth. Breathing deeply, imagine pulling energy up from the earth's core and connecting this energy with your feet. With each inhalation, you deepen this connection, seeing, sensing, or feeling this energy as a translucent red cord of light.

2. Once you have connected the energy with your feet, use your inhaled breaths to draw the energy up your legs and spine and to the crown of your head.

3. Now imagine there is a small opening at the crown. As you continue to inhale, send the red translucent energy rising up through the crown and visualize this energy bubbling up like a fountain of red water.

4. Imagine next that with your breaths you are pulling a translucent gold cord of energy down from the sun. See the energy coming down through the opening in your crown, traveling down your spine to your feet, and then to the core of the earth.

5. Now, for several minutes, sense the commingled red and gold energies repeatedly going up and down your spinal column.

6. With intention and breath, extend the energies and let them travel from your opened crown to your feet.

7. Last, extend and align your energies down to the earth's core and up to the sun's light with this expansive flow.

You have run your energy.

For a variation of this exercise, in Step 4 you may wish to envisage a translucent silver cord of energy pulled from the moon and stars.

The more willing you are to surrender
to the energy within you, the more
power can flow through you.

Shakti Gawain

Can you feel?

The purpose of asking yourself the questions below is to sharpen your focus and to develop sensory awareness, which, in turn, stills your mind. Doing so will help you relax, no matter how frazzled you may be. Try it. Find a quiet place and slowly repeat the questions.

Can you feel a soft breeze on your cheek?

Can you feel your bare feet walking on thick grass?

Can you feel the sensation of diving into cool water on a hot summer day?

Can you feel the sumptuousness of a piece of velvet?

Can you feel the softness of a dog's fur?

Can you feel your body getting heavier?

Can you feel a butterfly alight on your left shoulder?

Can you feel the warmth of the sun on your face?

Can you feel the rustle of wind next to your right ear?

Can you feel the comforting weight of an extra blanket on your body?

Can you feel the sun warming your toes?

Can you feel yourself sinking into a hot bath?

Can you feel the weight of the shoes or socks on your feet?

Can you feel the gentle beating of your heart?

Can you feel the weight of your body as it settles into a chair?

Can you feel the tension in your shoulders lessening?

Can you feel your breath becoming deeper?

Can you feel your hands becoming open and warm?

Can you feel the smoothness of your forehead?

Can you feel your legs becoming heavy?

Can you feel like a rag doll?

Can you feel the softness around your eyes?

Can you feel as if you are floating in salt water?

Can you feel yourself becoming longer?

Can you feel your breath becoming even deeper?

Can you, once again, feel like a rag doll?

Can you feel your eyes wanting to close?

Can you feel yourself relaxing?

Note: This exercise is particularly good for those of us who tend to hang out in our heads and might have a few control issues. If you like this exercise, consider recording this, giving a full 60 seconds between questions. This is a good, effective form of relaxation and a great precursor to meditation.

Tension is who you think you should be. Relaxation is who you are.

Chinese proverb

The greatest prayer is patience.

Buddha

Being resilient

Life can be challenging, full of unexpected events that turn your world upside down. Everything can go into a spin, and you can find yourself overwhelmed and feeling out of control. It can be hard to find your footing, much less get clearheaded on what you think or feel. To encourage your process, here are a few coping strategies to help you refind your balance and maintain equanimity.

MAINTAIN PERSPECTIVE and remember the long view. As with the eagle that flies high in the sky and looks down at the ground below, the long view widens your perspective and adds detachment. You step away from the immediate and are able to look at the whole.

Keep the faith in your ability to weather the storm and to find some resolution and healing in the challenges before you. Attitude and intention are potent energy medicine.

RELEASE THE EXCESS ENERGY and tension that make you tight, taut, tense, and cranky. You might be one to simmer, sit, stew, obsess, ruminate, nitpick, worry, fret, agonize, or perseverate. Your sleep may be disturbed; your eating might be off or very on. Your temper could be short; your fear might be long. You may feel as if you are unraveling. Most likely, you are experiencing sensory overload—too much bad news, too many demands, limited resources, too much to juggle, too much to shoulder.

You can discharge your excess energy in one of two ways: physical or expressive. The physical includes any kind of movement—exercise, walking, dancing, making love. The expressive is about releasing by way of a heart-to-heart talk, writing, singing, drawing, or other creative endeavor that funnels the excess energy out of your system. Once it has been drained, you will become more effective.

BREATHE. It sounds so basic. You do it every day—without thinking. However, a regular practice of a dozen deep breaths, a few times a day, can reground you in you, help you reconnect with your physical self and decrease stress. It's simple, and so easy to do. You oxygenate your body; you reinhabit yourself; and you become more clearheaded, less frazzled, and better able to deal with things. It can't hurt, and it works.

Follow Gandhi's advice: "Be the change you want to see."

IF YOU ACCEPT THAT EVERYTHING IS ENERGY, wouldn't it follow that every one of your actions is a kind of energetic input that affects not only your existence, but that of the world as well? Every action makes a difference. Quantum physics has proved this. Therefore, consider being your Highest Self and act with integrity; treat everyone like your brother or sister, work for peaceful and respectful resolutions; and offer a hand to help those in need. In doing this, you become a powerful agent of change that helps create the shift toward a more responsible, conscious, interconnected, and caring world.

To know enough is enough,
is enough to know.

Tao Te Ching

Those who love you are
not fooled by mistakes you
have made or dark images
you hold about yourself.
They remember your beauty
when you feel ugly; your
wholeness when you are
broken; your innocence
when you feel guilty; and
your purpose when you
are confused.

African saying

Healing the violent heart

From a soul perspective, we are all connected. We are all part of one pulsing, thrumming web of consciousness. Every act of violence, every act of kindness creates a kind of energetic force field. Our words and our actions influence the balance of consciousness in our planet.

Our world is awash in many unspeakable forms of brutality and violence. What can we do to heal the violent heart?

"LET THERE BE PEACE ON EARTH AND LET IT BEGIN WITH ME"

Peace, like happiness, is an inside job. We need to make peace with our warring factions, be they our inner critic, family members, or coworkers. We do that by ceasing the aggressive, critical attacks on ourselves and others; we do that by ending the harmful self-destruction that spirals out and influences others.

"HE AIN'T HEAVY, HE'S MY BROTHER"

We do not live in isolation. There are moments when we are called to carry others via an extended hand, a quick smile, or a heartfelt connection. If you accept that we all are connected, what you do for others, you do for yourself. And, sometimes, those other people are heavy, in the sense that their behavior is aberrant, odd, or crazy-making, and you are called to carry them. And you do—toward some person or place of help and healing.

INCREASE YOUR EQ

You have heard of IQ, intelligence quotient. There is also EQ, which stands for emotional quotient and relates to a person's ability to handle emotions. Can the person deal with stress? Find a safe outlet for expressing anger? Be resilient? Demonstrate kindness? Interact well with others? Research has proven that children with a higher EQ are more successful in life than those with a higher IQ. It makes sense that if you can navigate the emotional and, by extension, the social shoals of a group, you are going to fare better in the world than others who struggle emotionally and relationship-wise.

OPEN YOUR HEART

Kindness and compassion have been proven to change the energy, the vibe, if you will, of a situation.

They can counter negativity and hatred. They are energetic healing tools. Openhearted practices make an enormous difference by creating a bridge and making a connection. It takes some practice, but it's not so hard. If you choose to be peaceful with yourself and with others, if you choose to be authentic in your words and actions, if you learn how to healthily connect, to accept and express your emotions, and if you practice kindness and compassion, you can begin the process. You can heal the violent heart.

Compassion is based on the knowledge that the other person is fundamentally like you.

The Dalai Lama

Lovingkindness meditation

Lovingkindness meditation, known as *metta* meditation (*metta* is a Pali word for *friend*), is a classic Buddhist practice of goodwill. This practice is said to bring many benefits of peacefulness and protection. This is a deceptively simple practice in which you begin the focus on yourself and later direct your attention to others.

Here is what you do.

Beforehand: Say the four phrases (see below) to yourself and notice how you respond to each phrase. Practice getting comfortable with the words. Attend to yourself with an open, loving mind.

The practice:

1. Sit comfortably. You may close your eyes or simply have them go soft.
2. Be present to yourself as you inhale and exhale easy, full breaths.
3. Slowly think and say to yourself the four phrases of lovingkindness.

4. With attention and focus, slowly recite these phrases to yourself.

The meditation:

> May I feel safe.
> May I feel happy.
> May I feel strong.
> May I live with ease.

Notes:

You can do this practice sitting or, even, mindfully walking.

Ideally, practice for 10 minutes, twice a day.

When you feel ready, you can increase your practice to 20, and later 30, minutes a session, twice a day.

As you become more comfortable and fluent with this practice, you can amend the meditation in two ways:

1. Say this meditation for loved ones, for example:

> May Jane feel safe.
> May Jane feel happy.
> May Jane feel strong.
> May Jane live with ease.

2. For advanced lovingkindness practice, say this
   meditation for someone who is challenging to you
   in your life. It can put a whole new spin on your
   perspective.

With practice, you will notice changes in your reactions
and responses to life.

The heart that gives, gathers.
Tao Te Ching

Healing star

You are having one of those days. Everything has turned sour. You are at a loss for what to do next. You have little energy and little motivation to take the next step.

Try this: See yourself walking along a path, whatever comes to your mind easily. Now imagine that as you walk, you look down and see a tiny green metallic star—a perfectly shaped five-pointed star. Its shape and its color give you pause. You find this star uplifting for some unknown reason.

You bend down and pick it up. You hold it in your hand and smile at this mysterious occurrence in your not-so-pleasant day. It all feels a little magical, and today, of all days, you could be open to some magic.

As soon as you have this thought, the star begins to spin and expand. It becomes the size of a Ping-Pong ball and hovers at the midpoint of your breastbone. Clearly, this star has found you for a reason today.

Intuitively, you know what to do. You allow your breath to deepen and you focus on the rotating green star. As you breathe in, you take in the green energy of the star. You find it calming, soothing, and relaxing. As you breathe out, you release tightness and tension, pain and discomfort. You settle into a rhythm of deep star-focused breathing and discover that the more time you spend in this endeavor, the better you feel. You find yourself feeling lighter, more energetic and more balanced. The day has recovered some of its sweetness.

Today, consider a little magic, and take in some healing star energy.

Alice laughed. "There is no use trying," she said, "one can't believe impossible things." "I daresay you haven't had much practice," said the Queen. "When I was your age, I always did it for half-an-hour a day. Why, sometimes I've believed as many as six impossible things before breakfast."

Through the Looking Glass, by Lewis Carroll

How does one live with death?

Death is a physical, earthly matter. Death takes away breath and stops a heartbeat, the body no longer functions, the physical self ceases to exist.

For those loved ones left behind, death leaves residue; there are tears and runny noses. Death wracks a body with pain, steals the appetite, erases joy, and dampens desire. Death leaves a tangible stranglehold on the heart. Death pummels the survivor's body with cellular memory. Death hurts. No matter how prepared you think you are, death hurts.

Once the funeral is over and the relatives and friends have returned to their daily routines, the reality of the loss smacks you across the heart and you find yourself crying frequently. You pick up the phone to speak to the one you lost before you remember that's no longer possible. Songs on the radio, books on the shelf, a certain kind of soup, summer in the backyard—they all tug at you. You miss your loved one. You want him or her back. It was too soon; it was too fast. It is never the right time—or so it seems.

So, how does one live with death?

SLOWLY AND GENTLY

There are no set rules, so specific formulas. No two people grieve in the same way. Some walk the beach endlessly; others visit the cemetery. Some stay at home nested in dim light until they feel they can deal with the bright light of the world outside their door.

It takes time to absorb the loss. Be very gentle with yourself and allow yourself the space and the time to cry, or to even rant and rave at the injustice of it all.

FREQUENTLY TRAVEL MEMORY LANE

Revisit, remember, and hold dear what you have lost. Perhaps you read the same poem over and over or play the same CD repeatedly or go to bed wearing the sweater that still holds his or her scent.

Honor your loved one by remembering. In ancient times and in indigenous cultures, those who had passed before were revered and remembered for their wisdom, experience, and the unique gifts they shared with their family and community.

Take time to remember; it is a blessing for the ones who have passed.

BE LIKE WATER

Water is symbolically associated with emotions. Opening the heart and allowing the emotions to flow is part of the process. If you do not feel, then all those emotions stagnate, like water that doesn't move.

May I suggest that you be like water that moves in its own way, sometimes quiet and unobtrusive, other times raging. Allow yourself to flow, trickle, get dammed up, overflow, and swirl; be the currents, eddies, pools, and serpentine streams. Know yourself in all your watery forms; feel yourself as cold, hard ice; hot, vaporous steam; gently falling snow; coursing rain; and soft, glistening mist.

CHOOSE TO LIVE

In time, permit yourself to become like the wee sprout of green that has pushed its way through a crack in the concrete and is now facing the sunlight. See yourself having pushed through layers of weighted sadness and pain—having moved through those times when you felt you couldn't catch a full breath. Now, you are rooted, once again, in the earth and showing your face, albeit your fragile face, to the world. Honor your loved one with the gift of choosing to live your life fully.

There is no death,
only a change of worlds.
Chief Seattle

Quiet time

Have you ever considered creating a daily window for quiet time? Perhaps taking 30 minutes of unadulterated unscheduled time to sit quietly? Nothing fancy, simply 30 precious minutes with the telephone unplugged, the computer turned off, and no one permitted to disturb you.

This is time in which you unburden yourself. There is nothing to carry—no bags, books, briefcases, messages, worries, responsibilities, or chores. Everything is left outside the 30-minute circle but you.

In fact, you might envision drawing an imaginary circle around this dedicated space. It will provide you with boundaries—an energetic safety zone in which to release your cares and worries. By creating a temporary sanctuary in which you can refresh, recharge, and replenish yourself, you are free to be alone with your thoughts, stare into space, take a bath, meditate, or simply rest your eyes.

Being quiet is a healing endeavor; it soothes jangled nerves, pre-empts the bombardment of sensory stimulation, and allows the body to become still. It calms the energy field and provides restorative tranquillity to the mind-body. Being quiet is an avenue for balance and peace.

Being quiet also connects you with yourself. It gives you the opportunity to tune in to yourself and listen to what is bubbling beneath the surface; it gives you the space to sort out jumbled emotions or gnarled thoughts. It becomes a place where you can process and digest the knotted and the tangled. Being quiet allows you to clear out the internal clutter and approach the remainder of the day with a refreshed attitude. By regularly taking a mere 30 minutes a day for quiet time, you can create an oasis amid the hurry of your days.

Consider giving yourself permission to take a full 30 minutes of quiet. Sanctuary time calls you.

How beautiful it is to do nothing and then rest afterward.

Spanish proverb

Unleashing your soul

Our souls get ignored. We get busy and neglect to listen to our inner peanut gallery that needs a day at the beach, a night of music, a weekend of quiet, an article of beauty, or a satisfying read.

It happens. We get preoccupied. We do our thing. There are errands, chores, kids, parents, bills—life. And the days morph into months, and the months become years. We ignore those repeated small cries of protest that bubble up when we take a minute to breathe. We promise ourselves we'll create the space and take the time later. Later never happens, and so the struggle begins.

We find ourselves becoming more stressed, more conflicted because now we are battling ourselves. We want to be free of the unconscious restraints that wear away our happiness, joy, and satisfaction.

What would help?

Here are a few suggestions. They are not new, but they are time-tested and honored for their effectiveness.

TAKE A NAP

You're exhausted. I know you are. So stop, and allow yourself to rest.

A wise woman once told me that 90 percent of the problems in her family were resolved following a decent meal and a good night's sleep. She was right. We often have to return to the basics of self-care just to find our center. It takes courage to stop the wheels of motion and allow ourselves time to regroup and recoup, and as author Sue Monk Kidd says, "Stopping is a spiritual art."

GET QUIET

Nap time notwithstanding, we need time to be still and to stop the sensory overload and reconnect with ourselves. So much is thrown at us in a given day that it is hard to separate ourselves from it all. Consider the words of the poet Rumi: "Let the waters settle; you will see stars and moon mirrored in your Being." Isn't that a lovely thought? Think of our individual celestial bits surfacing in our psyche.

PAY ATTENTION

Our souls do communicate with us. They tell us what thrills and delights them. They nudge us with signs and symbols along the way. Ever have a book fall into your hands or at your feet, a book that turns out to be the perfect book for you at the moment? Ever been gifted with a CD and there is one song that sings to your soul, one you play repeatedly? Ever find your personal symbol being paraded in front of you with constant sighting of blue herons or lilies or specific times on a clock?

Carl Jung once said, "Whatever crosses my path violently or suddenly, I attribute to God." The liminal world abounds with magic and mystery. We can choose to ignore, or we can choose to attend to the messages swimming just under the radar waiting for our connection.

GET PASSIONATE

The juiciness of life, high-voltage enthusiasm, and deeply felt emotions speak to getting in touch with the rock 'n' roll of your soul. Simply stated, if you are passionate about what you do, you are most likely listening to the desires of your soul.

ACCEPT YOURSELF

How long does it take for us humans to finally accept all parts of ourselves, to forgive our transgressions and gaffes, and to operate from compassion? We struggle and struggle and struggle because there is some point, some facet, some aspect that we refuse to accept or forgive. We can be so hard on ourselves. Our souls yearn for reconciliation of the warring parts. Like the potted violet on the windowsill, our souls lean toward the light for growth.

LISTEN AND TRUST

Trust your soul's inclinations and allow yourself to unfold like the tight bud of a rose. See yourself unfolding, petal by petal, into your full bloom. There is no one like you on the planet; there is no one with your exact DNA and your exact backpack of experiences.

Your soul calls for you to remember who you are and to walk into your magnificence.

It's time. The world needs you.

Everything you want is out there waiting for you to ask. Everything you want wants you, but you have to take action to get it.

Jack Canfield

50 ways to feed your soul

The soul yearns for beauty, art, harmony, stillness, awe, a connection with the cosmos, communion with others, and moments of play. It desires illumination with all that makes us feel whole, a part of, and in the flow. The soul revels in joy and merrymaking; it delights in creative expression. The soul is nurtured by authentic and genuine responses. The soul lives in the moment.

Here are some suggestions for feeding your soul on this very busy Planet Earth.

1. Have a pillow fight.
2. Sit in the garden.
3. Wrap yourself in quietude.
4. Smell a rose.
5. Smell a baby.
6. Smell your lover's neck.
7. Surrender to love.

8. Surrender to silliness.

9. Think of possibilities.

10. Doodle.

11. Let go.

12. Let God.

13. Let someone else have a turn.

14. Watch a rainstorm.

15. Listen to beautiful music.

16. Pay it forward.

17. Dream with the moon.

18. Jump into a mound of leaves.

19. Take a walk in the snow.

20. Swim with the dolphins.

21. Walk in a forest.

22. Have your feet massaged.

23. Buy yourself flowers.

24. Enchant a child with a story.

25. Open your clown chakra.

26. Laugh and giggle; romp and play.

27. Stop.

28. Look at beauty.

29. Make something.

30. Forgive yourself—for everything.

31. Take a stroll at sunset.

32. Sing in the shower.

33. Dance in the kitchen.

34. Have a conversation by candlelight.

35. Play in the dirt.

36. Climb into your bed with clean sheets.

37. Bake bread.

38. Talk with your ancestors.

39. Take a morning for yourself.

40. Read before breakfast.

41. Climb to the top of the mountain.

42. Lend a hand.

43. Hold hands.

44. Fingerpaint.

45. Listen to the ocean.

46. Take a nap on the couch.

47. Take an aromatic bath.

48. Practice kindness.

49. Play with a puppy.

50. Be willing to learn the lessons that joy can teach.

*Put your ear down
close to your soul and listen hard.*

Anne Sexton

If ants are such busy
workers, how come they
find time to go to all
those picnics?

Marie Dressler

Acknowledgments

You know the expression; it takes a village ... That has most certainly been the case for the creation of this book. There have been so many people who have helped form me and helped me create a better book. I am so very grateful to all of you, and specifically:

Anne, Kevin, Little A—my BFF, and the Big Toot, for always being my greatest support and loudest cheering section; thank you for everything.

Elinor, for seeding my spiritual future; *in requiem vita.*

Marie, aptly identified as "Liquid Sunshine," for using your overqualified expertise as the best right hand and detail queen ever; for your friendship, tenacity, and support.

My family of friends—who have been with me throughout the decades—Annie and Kenny, Ginny, Heidi, Martha, Mary Swain, Nora, and Sharon—each of you has been with me through ups and downs, thick and thin. Oh, all the history, the fun, the conversations, the adventures, and the laughs we have shared. It has been, and will always be, a tremendous comfort and blessing to have each of you in my life.

Jennifer, Henry, and Guinness, for your enormous gift of time, space, and beauty at your cottage in Glastonbury, England, where this book began in the summer of 2006.

Anne and MMKK, for a soft spot to land in London and a sweet sanctuary where I could cross my t's, dot my i's, and catch my breath in the fall of 2010.

My fabulous editorial team from the UPI days and going forward: Larry "Larry in the conservatory with the pipe wrench" Moffitt, for opening the UPI writing door in 2006 with your encouragement, mentoring, and humor; Renee "Eagle Eye" Corley, for your exquisite sense of detail and editorial assistance; and Anne Harris, for your ability to see the big picture and for being a terrific friend. Thank you all; I now know why writers love their editors.

Editor and designer O. B. Crowder, you are a delight and you work magic. Thank you for doing the deed with this manuscript.

All my teachers—most especially Jeanne Achterberg, Ph.D., G. Frank Lawlis, Ph.D., Caroline Myss, Ph.D., C. Norman Shealy, M.D., Ph.D.— you helped form my thinking and my practice of psychotherapy.

My cognitive-behavioral gang, Susan Egelko, Ph.D., Steve Geschwer, Ph.D., Susan A. Mufson, C.S.W., and Bernard G. Pasquariella, M.A. We bonded at IBT in 1989, and my life has been enriched in countless ways since.

Elizabeth and Gayook, my fellow sojourners on the path, you have taught me so much by the power of your respective examples.

Last, but never least, each and every one of my clients, students, and mentees: you have been my best teachers; you have brought out my best self. None of this would have been possible without you.

About the author

Adele Ryan McDowell, Ph.D., is a psychotherapist with more than 30 years' experience, a teacher of meditation, intuition development, and higher consciousness, an internationally known workshop facilitator, and an energy healer. She was founder and director of The Greenheart Center, a holistic, psychoeducational center in Stamford, Connecticut, is the creator of Faithwalk[SM]: A psychospiritual approach to transformation, and founded and directed the Institute for the Study of Symbolic and Shamanic Energies. Her work integrates psychology with spirituality, helping clients move through crises and restore balance by accessing core soul issues. She is a perpetual student who believes in the power of an open heart and a good laugh.

You may learn more about Adele, her thinking, and her writing at *www.theheraldedpenguin.com* and *www.channeledgrace.com.*